# Interfaith Dialogue at the Grass Roots

# Interfaith Dialogue at the Grass Roots

EDITED BY
REBECCA KRATZ MAYS

ECUMENICAL PRESS
PHILADELPHIA, PENNSYLVANIA

Chapter 5, "Bringing the Dialogue Home," reproduced with permission of the publisher from *Opening the Covenant: A Jewish Theology of Christianity*, by Michael S. Kogan, © 2008 Oxford University Press, Inc.

ISBN-10: 0-931214-11-4
ISBN-13: 978-0-931214-11-0

Design and Layout: Glenn Ferrell and Rebecca Kratz Mays
Cover Art: *Laissez circuler l'Énergie* (2000), Isabelle Mougeot, used with permission of the artist.

*Printed in the United States of America.*

Ecumenical Press
Temple University (022-38)
1114 W. Berks St.
Philadelphia, PA 19122-6090

Dialogue Institute/
*Journal of Ecumenical Studies*
www.jesdialogue.org
dialogue@temple.edu

# Acknowledgments

*Interfaith Dialogue at the Grass Roots* is the fruition of the vision, funding, and labor of a dedicated team of people. We are most grateful to Sergio and Lora Mazza for their ambitious and foresighted vision and the funding to make it real.

Leonard Swidler graciously invited me to serve as a guest editor for this project to publish one collection to serve both as an issue of the *Journal of Ecumenical Studies* and a book for the trade market.

Thanks go to many people for their commitment to the project: Julie Sheetz-Willard served as coordinator for the project, infusing us with good will and helping to make sure we synchronized our efforts. Joe Stoutzenberger created the questions for reflection and suggestions for action that conclude each chapter. Nancy Krody kept us all faithful to the best of style and the highest of standards in her proofreading.

English and Publishing graduate students in the "Manuscript Editing" class at Rosemont (PA) College read chapters early on to help make the writing more accessible to people not involved in interreligious dialogue. Two of those students deserve special thanks for continued editing work: Cathrine Lata and Sarah Lemore.

Three graduate assistants gave hours of attentive skill to this project: Nicole Rietmann and Megan Shove for proofreading and Glenn Ferrell for graphic design and layout.

And, a final thanks to my family, Stuart, Anna, Daniel, and my parents, Dot and Gene Kratz, for their labor and love on behalf of this hope for authentic conversation.

—Rebecca Kratz Mays

# Contents

# *Preface*

## CAN INTERRELIGIOUS DIALOGUE MAKE A DIFFERENCE?

Leonard Swidler

Whenever I am asked the question, "Does the interreligious dialogue you are always talking about ever really make any difference?" I answer with a resounding, *Yes!* and proceed to tell him (it's always a he) about Macedonia.

We were holding our then latest Jewish-Christian-Muslim Trialogue (started in 1978—ten scholars from each religion from around the world participated) in Jakarta, Indonesia, in February, 2000, at the Presidential Palace when my friend and close colleague Paul Mojzes (born in Yugoslavia) received an overseas phone call from Boris Trajkovski, the new President of Macedonia—the then newest of the independent republics from former Yugoslavia. He told Paul that he had read about our Trialogue in Indonesia and asked whether we could come to his country next, since they desperately needed help, which he hoped we might be able to provide.

In fact, Macedonia was falling into civil war. The large majority—perhaps 70%—of the population was Christian Orthodox, but a sizeable minority—perhaps 27%—was Muslim. Most of the Orthodox were ethnically Slavic, and most of the Muslims were Albanian. The religions, especially the two large ones, were more part of the problem rather than the solution, for over the centuries they had never spoken *with* each other, only *at* each other, and then almost always in accusatory tones. And that was very much the case in 2000! They frequently added fuel to the fire.

With the help of President Trajkovski, Paul and I visited Skopje, the capital of Macedonia, in June, 2001, to meet with the President and the leaders of the five recognized religious communities: Orthodoxy, Islam, Catholicism, Protestantism, and Judaism. The most difficult to persuade to support a Trialogue were the Orthodox, for they had the most to lose, but we were eventually able to get all to agree to a Jewish-Christian-Muslim

Trialogue, scheduled for November, 2001.

Later that summer of 2001, however, the political and military situation deteriorated so badly that the Trialogue had to be postponed. After intervention by NATO troops that fall, Paul and I visited Skopje again and once more had to convince all the religious leaders to proceed with the Trialogue, then set for May, 2002.

We hoped that we could 1) draw a dozen or more Macedonian clergy to attend the Trialogue, and 2) persuade the Orthodox and Islamic theological seminaries to allow us to bring a team of one Jewish, one Christian, and one Muslim scholar to lecture at each of their seminaries. As the time for the Trialogue grew closer and the local religious leaders, especially the Orthodox and the Muslim, saw that significant international attention would be focused on this event and their country, they encouraged their clergy to come to the Trialogue, and as a result over 100 attended all four days.

An even more dramatic development took place when Paul and I received a response on the weekend during the Trialogue to our request to send a team of three from the Trialogue to lecture at the Orthodox seminary. They asked us whether we could bring the *whole Trialogue* from the hotel to their seminary the next day, Monday, and asked the Dean of the Islamic seminary to give a lecture at the same time. We quickly recovered from our astonishment and said that we would have to ask the Dean of the Islamic seminary. When we asked him, he said that we would lecture at the Orthodox seminary–if the Trialogue would come to his seminary on Tuesday, and the Dean of the Orthodox seminary would give a lecture at his seminary! Miracles happen! And so we had a handshake between the two Deans at the Orthodox and Islamic seminaries, much like the earlier handshake of Rabin and Arafat on the lawn of the White House.

But the miracles did not stop there. Late Monday might the leadership of the Trialogue was suddenly invited to a midnight dinner at the Orthodox Metropolitan's palace, at which a tripartite commitment was hammered out: 1) to establish a Council on Interreligious Cooperation appointed by the respective heads of communities; 2) for the heads of the religious communities, particularly the Orthodox and Islamic, to meet three or four times a year to discuss issues between the communities; and 3) for the Orthodox and Islamic theological schools to begin cooperating in teaching students about each other's religion.

In fact, these three commitments have subsequently been successfully carried out, 1) with exchanges of faculty lectures at the two seminaries and joint student projects even outside the academic year, 2) with the Council on Interreligious Cooperation's working diligently together with the Parliament on laws relating to religion, and 3) with the religious leaders meeting regularly with the President of the country. Even beyond those, the Council on Interreligious Cooperation organized an ongoing series of one-day training programs for imams, priests, and ministers in several of the larger towns of Macedonia, which have been very successful.

After the extraordinary success of the 2002 Skopje Trialogue, President Trajkovski felt encouraged to continue in the direction of fostering interreligious dialogue and launched the first Ohrid Conference on Interreligious Dialogue in 2003, to which 300 delegates came from around the world. Most fortunately, that initial Ohrid Conference on Interreligious Dialogue was continued by the current Prime Minister Nikola Gruevski in 2007, and plans are laid to continue it on into the future.

Most of those 300 delegates from around the world went back to their countries renewed in their hopes for the difference interreligious dialogue can make in achieving respect and peace. We Jews, Christians, and Muslims now live in a global village where every individual is faced with religious pluralism. We need to learn how to make real the respect and peace across religious boundaries in our own backyards.

Two examples from my own experience add to the many more from the authors in this collection. Years ago I participated in a program called "Living Room Dialogues."

A group of four Jewish couples and four Christian couples was invited to get to know each other as Christians and Jews. They arranged to take turns meeting once a month at a Jewish couple's home, then a Christian's, alternating each month. The beginning is always the toughest time. Most groups choose what for them feels simple and non-threatening. In this group, each person took a turn telling others about his or her own image of "the other," Jew or Christian, as he or she grew up. The simple genius of this starter is that there are no "wrong" answers. "This story" is the image I had of Christians or Jews when I was growing up—that's all. Limiting the sharing to lived experience gave the Jews or Christians the opportunity to "correct" the sometimes strange, perhaps even weird or "off the wall," images each had. Everyone could laugh at the distorted pictures we often hold of each other. The ice was broken.

A second grassroots experience happened at an interreligious dialogue day jointly organized by a number of local organizations. Early in the day the group discussed the ten commonsense guidelines for interreligious dialogue called the "Dialogue Decalogue" (reprinted here in Chapter 1). In the afternoon four of the participants put on a five-minute skit in which one of the "Commandments" was not being observed; the result was a loud shouting match—the opposite of dialogue. Everyone left that day with a very vivid *feel* for the importance of that particular guideline, if dialogue instead of debate was to take place.

Interfaith dialogue at the grass roots means, for me, doing the work described in this collection as if we were at home in our living rooms able to take turns in serving each other as host or guest. My hope is that this group of authors will meet you where you are and encourage you to help create many fruitful dialogues.

# Introduction

Forty religious seekers filled the worship room in the converted barn at Pendle Hill, the Quaker study center in Pennsylvania near Philadelphia. Rabbi Marcia Prager and I sat attentive to each person present as we read a verse from the Genesis creation story, interpreting its meaning from our Jewish and Christian perspectives. "God said: Let us make humankind, in our image, according to our likeness" (Genesis 1:26). We paused to consider the plural pronouns in the passage; Marcia offered commentary from the rabbinical tradition. We then entered into silence for others to speak. A Christian Quaker pastor from Kenya rose slowly to his feet. With respect for the diverse faith perspectives in our group, he spoke with reverence for his tradition and experience. He identified Jesus, as God's companion in creation, saying with God, "Let us make humankind in our image ..."

Encounters such as this one have become more and more commonplace in our pluralistic world. More than ever before, people now live and work with members of other religious traditions. With the click of a computer mouse, we are up close to "the other," the person who is unfamiliar or the custom that we don't understand. Religious congregations are increasingly seeking to engage others in more formal ways. How do we sustain respect and create peace with "the other" without doing harm to the sincerity of a human's striving to live a religious life? In the above instance and in many others, a respectful silence and mutual dialogue can help.

In the opening story at the moment we entered into silence, I could feel persons both soften and stiffen as the differing perspectives on a mutual sacred story hung in the air. The difference was so wide a gap that we chose to encounter the mystery of difference just by being quiet, suspending any further debate or pointed discussion for a time. A deep stillness and sense of peace filled the room as each person had space to ponder, not needing exact agreement or debate. After this time of quiet worship, we took up the next verse. After the class session, over lunch, many animated conversations arose from the quiet opportunity we had experienced.

When agreement seems impossible at worst or difficult at best, what assumptions and approaches can reconcile difference? All the stories in

1

this collection presume a reconciling and unconditionally loving God at the heart of our encounter with "the other." Based on this assumption, each author offers a contribution toward increasing patience, passion, and understanding in doing dialogue among persons of differing faith traditions. These authors come from long practice in facilitating such encounters and have come to use the word "dialogue" as does Leonard Swidler, religion professor at Temple University, in Philadelphia, whose pioneer work in the twentieth century has done much to promote interfaith activity. He defines dialogue as "a conversation on a common subject between two or more persons with differing views, the primary purpose of which is for each participant to learn from the other so that s/he can change and grow."

Swidler and the other authors in this collection are aware of the groundswell of interest and concern since 9/11 for what can ensue from the absence of dialogue. In assembling these essays, we hope to empower imams, rabbis, pastors, and their congregants to take up the work of interreligious dialogue as a peacemaking activity. We encourage the same intentional work among all religious traditions. For the sake of focus and accessibility, the authors in this collection build on the scholars' trialogues among the Abrahamic traditions—Judaism, Islam, and Christianity. We want to add many others than scholars to the team, including theologians, religious leaders, teenagers and young adults, educators, and congregants for the fruition of the labor. To that end, a less formal understanding of dialogue is encouraged in several chapters. "Conversation" replaces "dialogue" in order to emphasize how interreligious engagement can be more commonplace when some basic understandings are in place.

In Chapter One, "Understanding Dialogue," Leonard Swidler discusses the basic reasons for creating interfaith encounters, delineates ten guidelines for conducting them, and tells some of the story of what can happen for people who take up the dialogue. Then Miriam Therese Winter, in Chapter Two, "Doing Effective Dialogue—and Loving It," describes "circles of conversation" that help make the encounter safe and productive. She and the next author, Eboo Patel, agree that one of the best ways to conduct encounters is to tell stories as the major part of any conversation—most especially in the interfaith youth work Patel does. In Chapter Three, "Storytelling as a Key Methodology for Interfaith Youth Work," Patel and two of his co-workers, April Kunze and Noah Silverman, outline why and how storytelling works so well. Drawing on assumptions about spiritual formation, they help us to understand just how powerful a simple yet sincere conversation can be.

Then, in Chapter Four, "The Next Thing to Dialogue," Edith Howe and

S. Mark Heim discuss a good step to take to help start constructive conversations where a different use of stories happens; they outline in instructive detail how to organize a book study group, choose effective books, and open the conversations that can evolve from reading. How do we begin to learn to do this conversation with skill and with safety? Michael S. Kogan offers us a compelling model in Chapter Five, "Bringing the Dialogue Home," for how the home church or synagogue is a good starting place for doing grassroots interfaith work. By being rooted in our own tradition and knowing it well, we are better able to comprehend the depth of wisdom in a different tradition. Accordingly, then, we move toward a healthy pluralism where engaged contact can expand each person's faith and understanding without creating a sense of threat or loss of one's own particular faith. Khaleel Mohammed, in Chapter Six, "The Art of Heeding," then offers a frank, feisty, and refreshing appraisal of our attempts at this difficult enterprise. He calls us to humility within a renewed vigor of heeding what "the other," the person who represents the unknown and the unfamiliar to us, actually has to say with his or her words and life. Then, in Chapter Seven, "The Power of Hope," Racelle Weiman appeals to our inability to comprehend a God who allows for great suffering. In the face of the assault to our sensibilities of the history of the *Shoah*, she claims the power of interfaith work to inspire our hope as a religious people. She calls on each of the Abrahamic traditions represented in this collection to establish just and peaceful communities.

We want to create practices and programs for real differences to co-exist without the beast of fear devouring life, light, and laughter. We hope readers will continue the conversation these writers have started. All of us have had interfaith encounters, both organized and spontaneous. How do we conduct ourselves? Do we recognize our resistances and know how to engage or disengage with appropriate respect? Do we know how to respect the differences even when we don't want to change and to grow? If we want to grow and to change, can we do so safely without mockery or exploitation? Are understanding and tolerance enough? What else is needed? If our own beliefs are shaky, how can the encounter with difference strengthen our own faith without tearing down the other? After all these and other questions are pondered, how do we take responsibility for the most important one: Do we walk with Micah, the prophet, in doing justice, loving mercy, and walking humbly with our God?

We invite readers to engage this collection with eyes open to the possibilities for interfaith encounters in the churches, synagogues, and mosques in the neighborhoods where you live. We join you in sharing some of the questions and obstacles that we know arise when trying to do interfaith activities of any kind. We encourage trust in the assumption common to Judaism, Christianity, and Islam: Each of us is an equal before God, held in that reconciling and unconditional love and truthfulness we are intended to practice.

To encourage our practice, Joseph Stoutzenberger writes questions for reflection and suggestions for action at the end of each of the eight chapters. These questions and suggestions can be reframed and inspire different ones depending on each particular occasion for dialogue. Whatever our situation, Maria Hornung's conclusion guides us through three important exercises. First, she describes the many roles within a faith community participants can assume in order to facilitate interreligious engagement. Second, she places Swidler's "Dialogue Decalogue" in context. Finally, she draws on Swidler's stages of change in engaging interreligious dialogue in order to invite each of us to reflect on our own experiences.

This collection adds an epilogue. Why? Good conversation or fruitful dialogue grows out of real-life stories at the grass roots of our communities. After all the questions, suggestions, and discussions about interfaith dialogue, we wanted to share stories of grassroots dialogue as it happens. Achmad Munjid tells the story of his Indonesian people in their struggle to build a home for everyone. In his story, he refers often to the heart of interfaith dialogue happening when friendship is born. In the final story of the epilogue, Marcia Prager and I tell the story of our interfaith friendship, of how, out of each of our search within our own religious tradition for its depth, we found ourselves facilitating a Christian Quaker/Jewish interfaith dialogue. These closing stories of lived experience invite the telling of your own.

Each of us is needed in the work of religious reconciliation. We need many more persons who are skilled in interpreting our sacred texts; we need those who can lead worship with respect for differing practices; we need people who choose to build friendships with the joy of knowing "the other." When the needs are met, we befriend one another as followers of the one God. And perhaps, just maybe, we can catch a glimpse of the peace that is our inheritance as those followers.

*—Rebecca Kratz Mays*

Please send your suggestions and reflections to rgkmays@hotmail.com and/or Leonard Swidler at dialogue@temple.edu.

# Contributors

**S. Mark Heim** is the Samuel Abbot Professor of Christian Theology at Andover Newton Theological School in Newton Centre, MA. He has been deeply involved in issues of religious pluralism and Christian ecumenism. An ordained minister in the American Baptist Churches in the U.S.A, he represents that denomination on the Faith and Order Commissions of the World Council of Churches and the National Council of Churches of Christ in the U.S.A. Heim served for ten years on the Muslim-Christian Relations Committee of the National Council of Churches. He is the author of *Salvations: Truth and Difference in Religion* (Orbis, 1995), *The Depth of The Riches: A Trinitarian Theology of Religious Ends* (Eerdmans, 2001), and *Saved from Sacrifice: A Theology of the Cross* (Eerdmans, 2006), among other books. Heim received his B.A. from Amherst College, his M.Div. from Andover Newton, and his Ph.D. in theology from the Boston College-Andover Newton Joint Graduate Program. He is a member of the American Theological Society, the Christian Scholars of Judaism Group, and other professional organizations. In addition to the theology of religions and ecumenical theology, his research interests include science and theology, Baptist history, and global Christianity.

**Maria Hornung** is Coordinator for Interfaith Education at the Interfaith Center of Greater Philadelphia. She entered the Medical Mission Sisters in 1954, upon her graduation from Ursuline High School in New Orleans, LA. Following education as a pharmacist, she spent twenty-five years living in Africa in the countries of Uganda, Kenya, Nigeria, and Ghana. In her professional work she served as a pharmacist, hospital administrator, educator, and community leader and collaborated with people of many different faith traditions. During her last years in Africa she served as Sector Coordinator for the Medical Mission Sisters' mission in the African continent and as a member of its international governing council. From 1987 to 2003 she worked with new MMS members in North America and served as Sector Coordinator in North America. She received her M.Ed. (1970) and her M.A. (1995) in Interreligious Studies from Temple University. Her book, *Encountering Other Faiths*, was published by Paulist Press in 2007.

**Edith Howe** practiced law for twenty years before finding herself called to work in the area of interfaith dialogue. In response to the events of September 11, 2001, she formed the "Daughters of Abraham," a book group designed to foster mutual understanding among Muslim, Jewish, and Christian women. This group has met for over five years, and ten such groups have since been formed in the Boston and Washington, DC, areas. Howe is currently pursuing a master's of theology degree at Andover Newton Theological School in Newton Centre, MA, which shares a campus with the Hebrew College rabbinical school. She is an active member of the leadership team of Journeys on the Hill, an interfaith group formed by students at both schools. Journeys on the Hill has organized a number of interfaith events each semester, created an interfaith dialogue and study group, and prompted the offering of interfaith courses at the two schools.

**Michael S. Kogan** is Professor of Religious Studies and Chair of the Department of Philosophy and Religion at Montclair State University, Upper Montclair, NJ, where he has taught since 1973. He holds a B.A. in philosophy and a Ph.D. in religious studies from Syracuse University, with post-graduate study at the Jewish Theological Seminary of America and Columbia University. He serves on the Board of the *Journal of Ecumenical Studies,* the South Carolina Jewish Historical Society, and the Jewish Studies Program of the College of Charleston. In the fall of 2008 he will become Chair of the Program of Jewish-American Studies at Montclair State University. He has served as President of the Mid-Atlantic Region of the American Academy of Religion and is Director of the Schnitzer Institute of Adult Jewish Studies. Kogan writes and speaks widely in the field of Jewish-Christian theological dialogue, and, along with numerous articles, he has written *Opening the Covenant: A Jewish Theology of Christianity* (Oxford University Press, 2008), in which this essay first appeared.

**April Kunze** is the Vice-President of Programs at the Interfaith Youth Core, a Chicago-based international nonprofit organization to build the interfaith youth movement. Her reflections on interfaith youth work have inspired young people across the world and have appeared in over a dozen publications, including *Review and Expositor, Interreligious Insight, Buzz Magazine, Sourcepoint,* and *Awakening the Spirit, Inspiring the Soul.* Her professional background is in youth leadership, grassroots community-building, and organizational development. She is the founder and board chair of The Crib Collective, an organization focused on creating a culture of social entrepreneurship among Chicago youth. A graduate of Carleton College and Public Allies Chicago, Kunze was recently named Public Allies Chicago's Changemaker of the Year.

**Rebecca Kratz Mays** is a Quaker teacher and editor with a B.A. from Earlham College and an M.A. from the University of Pennsylvania. For ten years, she taught "Approaching the Gospels Together" at the Quaker adult study center, Pendle Hill, near Philadelphia, PA, and for twenty years she edited and managed Pendle Hill books and pamphlets. Currently, she directs the Master's Degree progam in English and Publishing at Rosemont College, Rosemont, PA. She is clerk for Friends Association for Higher Education, a consortium of Quaker colleges, universitites, and adult study centers. In her local congregation, West-town Monthly Meeting, she is clerk for the worship and ministry committee. She currently teaches Quaker faith and practice, facilitates retreats, and co-leads Christian Quaker/Jewish interfaith dialogue workshops with Rabbi Marcia Prager.

**Khaleel Mohammed** is Associate Professor in the Department of Religious Studies at San Diego (CA) State University. He received B.A.'s from Interamerican University (Religion and Psychology) and Imam Muhammad Bin Saud University (Islamic Law), an M.A. in History and Philosophy of Religion from Concordia University, and a Ph.D. in Islamic Law from McGill University. He was a Kraft-Hiatt Postdoctoral Fellow and Lecturer in Islamic Studies at Brandeis University's Department of Near Eastern and Judaic Studies (2001–03) and has served as visiting professor/lecturer in universities in Yemen, Syria, Canada, and the U.S. He has lectured and written extensively on Muslim-Jewish relations, with articles appearing in the *Middle East Quarterly, Islamic Studies, Social Science and Modern Society,* and the *Journal of Religion and Culture.*

**Achmad Munjid** was born to a traditional Muslim family in Central Java, Indonesia, where he was trained in Qur'ān, Hadith, and Islamic Law in a *pesantren* (traditional Islamic boarding school). He holds a B.A. (1999) in English and an M.A. in Comparative Religion from Gadjah Mada University, Indonesia. He is now a doctoral candidate in the Religion Department at Temple University, where he is researching the key Indonesian thinkers of interreligious dialogue. He has presented papers in various conferences and seminars held by American Muslim Social Scientists (AMSS), American Council for the Study of Islamic Societies (ACSIS), New Jersey Council for Humanities (NJCH), and Legacy International. He is now teaching as Adjunct Instructor in the Religion Department of Temple University as well as working as an Associate at The Dialogue Institute.

**Eboo Patel** is the founder and Executive Director of the Interfaith Youth Core in Chicago. He is the author of *Acts of Faith: The Story of an American Muslim—The Struggle for the Soul of a Generation*. Patel holds a doctorate in the sociology of religion from Oxford University, where he studied on a Rhodes scholarship. He writes "The Faith Divide," a featured blog on religion for *The Washington Post*, and has also written for *The Chicago Tribune, The Clinton Journal, The Harvard Divinity School Bulletin*, and National Public Radio. Patel serves on the Religious Advisory Committee of the Council on Foreign Relations, the National Committee of the Aga Khan Foundation USA, the Advisory Board of Duke University's Islamic Studies Center, and the Board of the Chicago History Museum. He has spoken at the Clinton Global Initiative, the Nobel Peace Prize Forum, and at universities around the world. Patel is an Ashoka Fellow, was named by *Islamica Magazine* as one of ten young Muslim visionaries shaping Islam in America, and has been profiled by PBS and several other media outlets.

**Marcia Prager** is a Jewish renewal rabbi, teacher, storyteller, and therapist. She is Director and Dean of Ordination Programs for ALEPH: Alliance for Jewish Renewal, and rabbi for the P'nai Or Jewish Renewal communities of Philadelphia, PA, and Princeton, NJ. Her book, *The Path of Blessing* (Bell Tower, 1998/Jewish Lights, 2003), is an exploration of the profound spiritual wisdom that lies in the Jewish practice of blessing. She is the creator of the unique P'nai Or Siddurim (prayerbooks) for Shabbat and other innovative approaches to prayer and liturgy. Her work as a teacher of Jewish spiritual practice includes developing and co-directing the Davvenen Leadership Training Institute at Elat Chayyim Jewish Spiritual Retreat Center in New York. She and her husband Hazzan Jack Kessler travel widely to teach in an array of Jewish and interfaith settings.

**Noah Silverman** serves as content coordinator within the Outreach Education and Training Team at the Interfaith Youth Core. He graduated Phi Beta Kappa with a B.A. in religious studies and international relations from Connecticut College, where he wrote his undergraduate thesis on interreligious peace-building in Israel/Palestine. He has worked for the World Conference of Religions for Peace at the United Nations, the Interfaith Encounter Association in Jerusalem, and the Council for a Parliament of the World's Religions in Chicago, including staffing the 2004 Parliament of the World's Religions in Barcelona. A Chicago native, Silverman grew up attending K.A.M. Isaiah Israel congregation in the South Side neighborhood of Hyde Park.

**Joseph Stoutzenberger** is Professor of Religious Studies at Holy Family University in Philadelphia, PA. He earned his M.A. in Religious Education at Loyola University in Chicago, and received his Ph.D. in Religion from Temple University. He has written and revised numerous high school textbooks in religious studies, and his most recent publications are *You Are My Friends: Gospel Reflections for Your Spiritual Journey* and *The Human Quest for God: An Overview of World Religions*, both published by Twenty-Third Publications. He has been involved in interreligious dialogue for many years, especially in the Philadelphia area.

**Leonard Swidler** is Professor of Catholic Thought and Interreligious Dialogue in the Religion Department at Temple University, where he has taught since 1966. He is Founder and President of the Dialogue Institute (Interreligious, Intercultural, International), as well as founding editor, together with his wife Arlene, of the *Journal of Ecumenical Studies*. At Temple, and as a visiting professor at universities around the world—including Graz, Austria; Tübingen, Germany; Fudan University, Shanghai; and the University of Malaya,

Kuala Lumpur—Swidler has mentored a generation of U.S. and international scholars in the work of interreligious dialogue. He holds degrees in history, philosophy, and theology from Marquette University (M.A.), Tübingen University (S.T.L.) and the University of Wisconsin (Ph.D.). Swidler has published more than 180 articles and 70 books, including: *Jewish-Christian-Muslim Dialogue* (1978); *Religious Liberty and Human Rights* (1986); *After the Absolute: The Dialogical Future of Religious Reflection* (1990); *A Bridge to Buddhist-Christian Dialogue* (1990); *Muslims in Dialogue: The Evolution of a Dialogue over a Generation* (1992); and *Trialogue: Jews, Christians, and Muslims in Dialogue* (co-edited with K. Durán and R. Firestone) (2007).

**Racelle Weiman** is Executive Director of the Dialogue Institute (Interreligious, Inter-cultural, International) at Temple University. She holds a B.A. in Jewish Studies from U.C.L.A. and an M.A. and Ph.D. from Temple University in the field of Interreligious Studies, specializing in the Holocaust and Interfaith Relations. She received accreditation in mediation at the Truman Peace Institute at Hebrew University, Jerusalem, and pursued postdoctoral research on ethnic conflict-resolution and the religious elements of conflict at the Fletcher School of Diplomacy at Tufts University (1995) and the Program on Negotia-tion at Harvard University (1997). Prior to her current appointment, she served as founding Director of the Center for Holocaust and Humanity Education, Hebrew Union College-Jewish Institute of Religion, Cincinnati, OH (2000–06). She has lectured at Haifa Univer-sity (1986–2000), where she taught and developed projects relating to tolerance education, prejudice reduction, and Holocaust and genocide studies. She held a research fellowship on Professional Ethics at the S. Neaman Institute and served on the production team of television documentaries including the Emmy-nominated *Finding Family*. She has written numerous textbooks and co-authored curriculum and teacher-training materials.

**Miriam Therese Winter** is professor of liturgy, worship, spirituality, and feminist stud-ies at Hartford Seminary in Connecticut, an international center for interfaith dialogue. An advocate of experiential learning as a gateway to interfaith relations, she has been active in ecumenical, interfaith, and cross-cultural contexts for many years. As a member of the international congregation of Medical Mission Sisters, she has taught throughout Africa, Asia, Australia, Europe, and Latin America. In the 1970s she spent three summers as a faculty member of an interfaith initiative in Jerusalem. Her Folk Mass was premiered at Carnegie Hall in the first ecumenical-interfaith concert in the history of the Hall. Her folk-style songs and contemporary hymns continue to be sung by communities of faith around the world. She has written a number of books on feminist ritual and spirituality and has been inducted into the Connecticut Women's Hall of Fame. Winter has a Ph.D. from Princeton Theological Seminary and several honorary doctorates from Roman Catholic universities.

# 1

# UNDERSTANDING DIALOGUE
Leonard Swidler

## I. THE DIALOGUE OF HEAD, HANDS, AND HEART

### The Universe Is a Cosmic Dance of Dialogue.

Dialogue—the mutually beneficial interaction of differing components—is at the very heart of the Universe, of which we humans are the highest expression: from the basic interaction of *matter and energy* (in Einstein's unforgettable formula: e=mc²—energy equals mass times the square of the speed of light), to the creative interaction of *protons and electrons* in every atom, to the vital symbiosis of *body and spirit* in every human, through the creative dialogue between *woman and man*, to the dynamic relationship between *individual and society*. Thus, the very essence of our humanity is dialogical, and a fulfilled human life is the highest expression of the *cosmic dance of dialogue.*

In the early millennia of the history of humanity we spread outward from our starting point in central Africa, and the forces of divergence were dominant. Because we live on one globe, however, we eventually began to encounter each other more and more frequently. Now the forces of stunning convergence are dominant.

During the era of divergence, we could live in isolation from each other; we could ignore each other. Now, in this era of convergence, we are forced to live in one world. We increasingly live in a global village. We cannot ignore "the other," the person who is different or the custom that is unfamiliar. Too often in the past we have tried to make over "the other" into a likeness of ourselves, often by violence. But this violence is the very opposite of dialogue. This egocentric arrogance is in fundamental opposition to the *cosmic dance of dialogue.* It is not creative; it is destructive.

Hence, we humans today have a stark choice: dialogue or death.

9

## Dialogue of Head, Hands, and Heart

Because we humans are self-reflecting/correcting beings, we are capable of self-transforming dialogue. There are for us four main dimensions to this activity of dialogue that correspond to the structure of our humanness: Dialogue of the Head, Dialogue of the Hands, Dialogue of the Heart, Dialogue of (W)Holiness.

*The Cognitive or Intellectual: Seeking the Truth*
In the "Dialogue of the Head" we mentally reach out to "the other" to learn from those who think differently from us. We try to understand how they see the world and why they act as they do. The world is far too complicated for any of us to understand alone; we can increasingly understand reality only with the help of "the other," in dialogue. This enlarged understanding is very important, because how we understand the world determines how we act in the world.

*The Illative or Ethical: Seeking the Good*
In the "Dialogue of the Hands" we join together with others to work to make the world a better place in which we all must live together. Since we can no longer live separately in this one world, we must work jointly to make it not just a house, but a home for all of us to live in. In other words, we join hands with "the other" to heal the world. The world within us, and all around us, always is in need of healing, and our deepest wounds can be healed only together with "the other," only in dialogue.

*The Affective or Aesthetic: Seeking the Beautiful*
In the "Dialogue of the Heart" we open ourselves to receive the beauty of "the other." Because we humans are body and spirit or, rather, body-spirit, we give bodily-spiritual expression in all the arts to our multifarious responses to life: joy, sorrow, gratitude, anger, and, most of all, love. We try to express our inner feelings, which grasp reality in far deeper and higher ways than we are able to put into rational concepts and words; hence, we create poetry, music, dance, painting, architecture—the expressions of the heart. All the world delights in beauty, and so it is here that we find the easiest encounter with "the other," the simplest door to dialogue.

*(W)Holiness: Seeking the One*
We humans cannot long live a divided life. If we are even to survive, let alone flourish, we must "get it all together." We must live a whole life. In a way there is a fourth "H" here, if we play a little with our English

word "whole," for it is pronounced as "hole." Indeed, this is what the religions of the western tradition mean when they say that we humans should be holy. We humans are not dis-integrated beings. Rather, we can be truly human only if we bring our various parts together in harmony, if we integrate our being holistically. Therefore, we are authentically human only when our multiple elements are in dialogue with each other, and we in turn are in dialogue with the others around us. We must dance together the "Dialogue of the Head," the "Dialogue of the Hands," and the "Dialogue of the Heart" within the *(W)Holy Cosmic Dance of Dialogue.*

Those who know western Medieval Philosophy will recognize that these are the "Metaphysicals," the four aspects of *Being* itself perceived from different perspectives: the One, the True, the Good, the Beautiful.

## II. WHAT IS DIALOGUE?

### The Meaning of Dialogue

Dialogue is a two-way communication between persons who hold significantly differing views on a subject, with the purpose of learning more truth about the subject from the other. Dialogue is not the process of imparting truth, however gently and kindly, to the ignorant. Dialogue must include a common understanding that no one side has a monopoly on the truth on any given subject.

We are, of course, in this context speaking about a particular kind of dialogue, namely, interreligious dialogue in the broadest sense, that is, dialogue on a religious subject by persons who understand themselves to be in different religious traditions and communities. If religion is understood as an "explanation of the ultimate meaning of life and how to live accordingly," then that would include all such systems even though they customarily would not be called religions but, rather, ideologies, such as atheistic Humanism and Marxism; hence, it is more accurate to speak of both interreligious and interideological dialogue.

### Why Dialogue Arose

One can, of course, justifiably point to a number of recent developments that have contributed to the rise of dialogue: growth in mass education and communications and travel; a world economy; and the threat of global destruction; nevertheless, a major underlying cause is a paradigm-shift in the West in how we perceive and describe the world. A paradigm is the model, the cluster of assumptions, on whose basis phenomena are perceived and explained; for example, the geocentric paradigm for explaining the movements of the planets. A shift to another paradigm—as to the heliocentric—will have a major impact. Such a paradigm-shift has occurred and is still occurring in the western understanding of truth statements, which has made dialogue not only possible but even necessary.

Whereas the understanding of truth in the West was largely absolute, static, monologic, or exclusive up to the last century, it has subsequently become deabsolutized, dynamic, and dialogic—in a word: relational.

All statements about reality are now seen to be related to the historical context, intentionality, perspective, language, and interpretation of the speaker, and in that sense no longer "absolute." Therefore, if my perception and description of the world are true only in a limited sense, that is, only as seen from my place in the world, then if I wish to expand my grasp of reality I need to learn from others what they know of reality that they can perceive from their place in the world that I cannot see from mine. That, however, can happen only through dialogue.

## Who Should Dialogue

Dialogue should involve every level of the religious, ideological communities, from the official representatives and experts in the various traditions to the "persons in the pews." Only in this way will the religious, ideological communities learn from each other and come to understand each other as they truly are.

What is needed for dialogue participants then is 1) an openness to learn from the other, 2) knowledge of one's own tradition, and 3) an equally disposed and knowledgeable dialogue partner from the other tradition. This exchange can happen on almost any level of knowledge and education. The key is the openness to learn from the other.

## Kinds of Dialogue

The three kinds or levels of dialogue are 1) ideas and words, 2) joint action or collaboration, and 3) prayer or sharing of the spiritual or depth dimension of our traditions. While the intellectual and verbal communication is indeed the primary meaning of dialogue, it will prove sterile if the results do not spill over into the other two areas of action and spirituality.

Serious involvement in joint action and/or spirituality will tend to challenge the previously held intellectual positions and lead to dialogue in the cognitive field. Catholic and Protestant clergy, for example, who found themselves together in concentration camp Dachau because of joint resistance to one or another Nazi anti-human action, began to ask each other why they did what they did and through dialogue were surprised to learn that they held many more positions in common than positions that separated them. In fact, these encounters and others like them fostered the Una Sancta Movement in Germany, which in turn was the engine that moved the Catholic Church in the Second Vatican Council (1962–65) to embrace ecumenism and interreligious dialogue after many centuries of vigorous official rejection.

Encountering our partner on merely one or two levels will indeed be authentic dialogue, but, given the integrative and comprehensive nature of religion and ideology, it is only natural that we be led from dialogue on one level to the others. Only with dialogue in this full fashion on all three levels will our interreligious, interideological dialogue be complete.

## Goals of Dialogue

The general goal of dialogue is for each side to learn and to change accordingly. Naturally, if each side comes to the encounter primarily to learn from the other, then the other side must teach, and thus both learning and teaching occur. We gradually learn more and more about our partners in the dialogue and in the process shuck off any misinformation about them. Our dialogue partner likewise becomes for us something of a mirror in which we perceive ourselves in new ways.

This expanded knowledge of ourselves and of "the other" cannot, of course, remain ineffective in our lives. As our self-understanding and understanding of those persons and things around us change, so too must our attitude and behavior toward ourselves and others change. To repeat: The goal of dialogue is that each side learn and change accordingly.

We need to learn first and as fully as possible the things we share in common with our dialogue partners, which most often will be much more extensive than we could have anticipated; we will thus be drawn together in greater harmony. Then, we learn more comprehensively what our differences are. Such differences may be 1) complementary, as, for example, a stress on the prophetic rather than the mystical; 2) analogous, as, for example, the notion of God in the Semitic religions and of *sunyata* in Mahayana Buddhism; or 3) contradictory, where the acceptance of one entails the rejection of the other, as, for example, the Judeo-Christian notion of the inviolable dignity of each individual person and the now largely disappeared Hindu custom of *suttee*, widow-burning. The issue of the third category of differences will be discussed below. The differences in the first two categories are not simply to be perceived and acknowledged; they should be cherished and celebrated both for their own sakes. By discerning them we have extended our own understanding of reality and how to live accordingly—the main goal of dialogue.

## The Means of Dialogue

A great variety of means and techniques of dialogue have been used successfully, and doubtless some are yet to be developed. Techniques that have already been utilized range from joint lectures and dialogues by experts from different traditions that are listened to by large audiences on one extreme to personal conversations between "rank and file" individuals from different traditions on the other.

In planning for any dialogue, the following issues deserve attention:

1) Use your creative imaginations and your sensitivity for persons.

2) Select representatives from all the traditions to be engaged in a dialogue, and involve them in its initial planning. This is particularly true when different communities first begin to encounter each other. Then dialogue about the potential dialogue itself becomes an essential part of the dialogic encounter.

3) In the first encounters between communities, the most difficult points of differences should not be tackled. Rather, those subjects that show promise of highlighting commonalities should be treated so that mutual trust between the partners can be established and developed.

4) Each partner is to come to the dialogue with total sincerity and honesty.

5) Care must be taken to compare our ideals with our partner's ideals and our practices with our partner's practices. By comparing our ideals with our partner's practices we will always "win," but we will learn nothing—a total defeat of the purpose of dialogue. For example, the Hindu custom mentioned above, the burning of live widows, *suttee*, is not to

be compared with the Christian commitment to the dignity of each individual life but to the centuries-long Christian practice (fortunately now abandoned) of burning witches.

6) Each partner in the dialogue must define her or himself; only a Muslim, for example, can know from the inside what is means to be a Muslim, and this self-understanding will change, expand, and deepen as the dialogue develops, and hence can be accurately described only by the one experiencing the living, growing religious reality.

7) Each partner needs to come to the dialogue with no fixed assumptions as to where the authentic differences between the traditions are; only after following the partner with sympathy and agreement as far as one can without violating one's own integrity will the true point of difference be determined.

8) Of course, only equals can engage in full, authentic dialogue.

9) Each partner is to come with a self-critical attitude toward himself or herself and the religious tradition he or she represents. Given that the primary goal of dialogue is to learn, to grow, and to change, we need to be willing to divest ourselves of a position we take should the dialogue reveal important reasons to do so.

10) The most fundamental means to dialogue is to have a clear expectation of the primary goal of the engagement: a two-way communication so that both partners can learn from each other and change accordingly.

## The Subject of Dialogue

Three main subject areas of dialogue include the *cognitive, active,* and *spiritual.*

The *cognitive* area holds the greatest range of possible subjects. It is almost unlimited—remembering the caution that the less difficult topics be chosen first and the more difficult later. Every dialogue group should nevertheless be encouraged to follow creatively its own inner instinct and interests. Some groups will start with more particular, concrete matters and then be gradually drawn to discuss the underlying issues and principles. Others will begin with more fundamental matters and eventually be drawn to reflect on more and more concrete implications of the basic principles already discovered. In any case, if proper preparation and sensitivity are provided, no subject should *a priori* be declared off-limits.

In the *active* area dialogue has to take place on the underlying principles for action that motivate each tradition. Once again many similarities will be found, as well as differences that will prove significant in determining the communities' differing stands on various issues of personal and social ethics. It is only by carefully and sensitively locating those underlying ethical principles for decision-making that later misunderstandings and unwarranted frustrations in specific ethical issues can be avoided. Then specific ethical matters, such as sexual ethics, social ethics, ecological ethics, or medical ethics can become the focus of interreligious, interideological dialogue—and ultimately joint action can take place where it has been found congruent with each tradition's principles and warranted in the concrete circumstances.

In some ways the *spiritual* area would seem to be the most attractive, at least to those with a more interior, mystical, psychological bent. Moreover, it promises a very great degree of commonality: The mystics appear to all meet together on a high level of unity with the Ultimate Reality no matter how it is described, including even in the more philosophical systems such as Neoplatonism. For instance, the greatest of the Muslim Sufis, Jewish Kabbalists, Hindu Bhaktas, Christian Mystics, Buddhist Bodhisattvas, and Platonist Philosophers all seem to be at one in their striving for and experience of unity with the One, which in the West is called God, *Theos*. At times the image is projected of God's being the peak of the mountain that all humans are climbing by way of different paths. Each one has a different way (*hodos* in Christian Greek, *halachah* in Jewish Hebrew, *shar'ia* in Muslim Arabic, *marga* in Hindu Sanskrit, *magga* in Buddhist Pali, *tao* in Chinese Taoism) to reach *Theos*, but all are centered on the one goal. Consequently, such an interpretation of religion or ideology is called theocentric.

Attractive as is theocentrism, one must be cautious not to waive the varying understandings of God aside as if they were without importance; they can make a significant difference in human self-understanding and hence how we behave toward ourselves, each other, the world around us, and the Ultimate Source. Moreover, a theocentric approach has the disadvantage of not including nontheists in the dialogue. This would exclude not only atheistic Humanists and Marxists, but also nontheistic Theravada Buddhists, who do not deny the existence of God but rather understand ultimate reality in a nontheistic, nonpersonal manner (theism posits a "personal" God, *Theos*). One alternative way to include these partners in the dialogue, even in this area of "spirituality," is to speak of the search for ultimate meaning in life, for "salvation" (*salus* in Latin, meaning a salutary, whole, [w]holy life; similarly, *soteria* in Greek), as what all humans have in common in the "spiritual" area, theists and nontheists. As a result, we can speak of a soteriocentrism.

## When to Dialogue—and When Not

In principle, of course, we ought to be open to dialogue with all possible partners on all possible subjects, at least until we learn where our true differences lie.

In this matter of differences, however, we have to be very careful in the distinctions we need to make. As pointed out above, in the process of the dialogue we will often learn that what we thought were real differences in fact turn out to be only apparent differences; different words or misunderstandings merely hid commonly shared positions. When we enter dialogue, however, we have to allow for the possibility that we will ultimately learn that on some matters we will find not a commonality but an authentic difference. These authentic differences can be of three kinds: complementary, analogous, or contradictory.

Complementary authentic differences will of course be true differences, but not such that only one could be valid. Furthermore, we know from our experience that the complementary differences will usually far outnumber the contradictory. Similarly, learning of these authentic but complementary differences will not only enhance our knowledge, but it also may very well lead to the desire to adapt one or more of our partner's complementary differences for ourself. As the very term indicates, the differences somehow complete each other, as the Chinese Taoist saying puts it: *Xiang fan xiang cheng* (Contraries complete each other).

We must not too easily and quickly place our true differences in the contradictory category. Perhaps, for example, Hindu *moksha*, Zen Buddhist *satori*, Christian "freedom of the children of God," and the Marxist "communist state" could be understood as different, but nevertheless analogous, descriptions of true human liberation. In speaking of true but analogous differences in beliefs or values here, we are no longer talking about discerning teachings or practices in our partner's tradition that we might then wish to appropriate for our own tradition. We are speaking of a difference that operates within the total organic structure of the other religion-ideology and that fulfills its function properly only within it. These real but analogous differences in beliefs or values should be seen not as in conflict with one another but as parallel in function and, in that sense, analogous.

At times, though, we can find contradictory truth claims, value claims, presented by different religious-ideological traditions. That happens, of course, only when they cannot be seen as somehow ultimately different expressions of the same thing (a commonality) or as complementary or analogous. When it happens, however, even though it be relatively rare, a profound and unavoidable problem faces the two communities: What should be their attitude and behavior toward each other? Should they remain in dialogue, tolerate each other, ignore each other, or oppose each other? This problem is especially pressing in matters of value judgments. What, for example, should the Christian (or Jew or Muslim or Marxist) have done in face of the now largely (but unfortunately not entirely) suppressed Hindu tradition of *suttee*? Should he or she try to learn its value, tolerate it, ignore it, oppose it (in what manner)? What about the Nazi tenet of killing all Jews? These, however, are relatively clear issues, but what of a religion-ideology that approves slavery, as Christianity, Judaism, and Islam did until a century ago? Maybe that is clear enough today, but what of sexism—or only a little sexism? Or what about the claim that only through capitalism—or socialism—can human liberation be gained? Making a decision on the proper stance becomes less and less clear-cut. At times, the choice to oppose a position or practice may be the peacemaking choice; even then the skills of deep listening and the willingness to change may be all important.

Eventually it was clear to most non-Hindus in the nineteenth century that the proper attitude was not to dialogue with Hinduism on *suttee*, but to oppose the practice. Apparently it was not so clear to all non-Nazis that opposition to Jewish genocide was the right stance to take. Furthermore, it took Christians almost 2,000 years to come to the conclusion to abolish slavery. Many religions and ideologies today stand in the midst of a battle over sexism, some even refusing to admit the existence of the issue. Lastly, no argument need be made to point out the controversial nature of the contemporary capitalism-socialism issue.

Obviously, important contradictory differences between religions-ideologies do exist and at times warrant not dialogue, but opposition. Individually, we also make critical judgments on the acceptability of positions within our own traditions and, rather frequently, within our personal lives. But certainly this exercise of our critical faculties is not to be limited to ourselves and our tradition; this perhaps most human of faculties should be made available to all—with all the proper constraints and concerns for dialogue already detailed at length. Of course, it must first be determined on what grounds we can judge whether a religious-ideological difference is in fact contradictory, and then, if it is, whether it is of sufficient importance and of a nature to warrant active opposition.

**Full Human Life**

Because all religions and ideologies are attempts to explain the meaning of human life and how to live accordingly, it would seem that those doctrines and customs that are perceived as hostile to human life are not complementary or analogous but contradictory and that opposition should be proportional to the extent they threaten life. What is to be included in an authentically full human life, then, must be the measure against which all elements of all religions-ideologies must be tested as we make judgments about whether they are harmonious, complementary, analogous, or contradictory—and then act accordingly.

What in this century has been acknowledged as the foundation of being human is that human beings ought to be autonomous in their decisions—such decisions being directed by their own reason and limited only by the same rights of others. Though frequently resistant in the past, and too often still in the present, the great religious communities of the world have likewise often and in a variety of ways expressed a growing awareness of and commitment to many of the same notions of what it means to be fully human. Hence, through dialogue humanity is painfully, slowly creeping toward a consensus on what is involved in an authentically full human life. The 1948 United Nations' *Universal Declaration of Human Rights* was an important step in that direction. Of course, much more consensus needs to be attained if interreligious, interideological dialogue is to reach its full potential.

The conclusion from these reflections, I believe, is clear: Interreligious, interideological dialogue is absolutely necessary in our contemporary world. We will not achieve our full potential for a full human life without learning to practice authentic dialogue.

## III. THE DIALOGUE DECALOGUE

**Ground Rules for Interreligious, Interideological Dialogue**

The following suggestions are not theoretical rules, or commandments given from "on high," but ones gleaned from hard experience. In the religious-ideological sphere in the past, we came together to discuss with those differing with us, for example, Catholics with Protestants, either to defeat an opponent, or to learn about an opponent so as to deal more effectively with her or him, or at best to negotiate with him or her. If we faced each other at all, it was in confrontation—sometimes more openly polemically, sometimes more subtly so, but always with the ultimate goal of defeating the other, because we were convinced that we alone had the absolute truth.

But dialogue is not debate. In dialogue each partner must listen to the other as openly and sympathetically as s/he can in an attempt to understand the other's position as precisely and, as it were, as much from within, as possible. Such an attitude automatically includes the assumption that at any point we might find the partner's position so persuasive that, if we would act with integrity, we would have to change, and change can be disturbing.

Minimally, the very fact that I learn that my dialogue partner believes "this" rather than "that" proportionally changes my attitude toward her; and a change in my attitude is a significant change in me. We do not enter dialogue to change the other's point of view as one hopes to do in debate. Because in dialogue each partner comes with the intention of learning and changing himself, one's partner ironically will usually grow and change. Thus the goal of debate, and much more, is accomplished far more effectively by dialogue.

How, then, can we engage in this activity to speak and listen well so as to render growth and change less disturbing? The following are some basic ground rules that will ensure effective dialogue.

**FIRST COMMANDMENT:** *The primary purpose of dialogue is to learn, that is, to change and grow in the perception and understanding of reality, and then to act accordingly.*

**SECOND COMMANDMENT:** *Interreligious, interideological dialogue must be a two-sided project—within each religious or ideological community and between religious or ideological communities.*

Because of the "corporate" nature of interreligious dialogue, and since the primary goal of dialogue is that each partner learn and change himself, it is also necessary that each participant enter into dialogue not only with his partner across the faith line—the Lutheran with the Anglican, for example—but also with his coreligionists, with his fellow Lutherans, to share with them the fruits of the interreligious dialogue. Only thus can the whole community eventually learn and change, moving toward an ever more perceptive insight into reality.

**THIRD COMMANDMENT:** *Each participant must come to the dialogue with complete honesty and sincerity.*

No false fronts have any place in dialogue. Any participant needs to be clear in what direction the major and minor thrusts of the tradition move, what the future shifts might be, and, if necessary, where the participant has difficulties with her own tradition.

*Conversely, each participant must assume a similar complete honesty and sincerity in the other partners.* Not only will the absence of sincerity prevent dialogue from happening, but the absence of the assumption of the partner's sincerity will do so as well. In brief: no trust, no dialogue.

**FOURTH COMMANDMENT:** *In interreligious, interideological dialogue we must not compare our ideals with our partner's practice.*

We must compare our ideals with our partner's ideals, our practice with our partner's practice.

**FIFTH COMMANDMENT:** *Each participant must define himself.*

Only the Jew, for example, can define what it means to be a Jew. Because dialogue is a dynamic medium, as each participant learns, he will change and hence continually deepen, expand, and modify his self-definition as a Jew—being careful to remain in constant dialogue with fellow Jews. Thus it is mandatory that each dialogue partner define what it means to be an authentic member of his own tradition.

*Conversely—the one interpreted must be able to recognize herself in the interpretation.* This is the golden rule of interreligious hermeneutics, as has been often reiterated by the "apostle of interreligious dialogue," Raimundo Panikkar. For the sake of understanding, each dialogue participant will naturally attempt to express for herself what she thinks is the meaning of the partner's statement; the partner must be able to recognize herself in that expression. The advocate of "a world theology," Wilfred Cantwell Smith, would add that the expression must also be verifiable by critical observers who are not involved.

**SIXTH COMMANDMENT:** *Each participant must come to the dialogue with no hard-and-fast assumptions as to where the points of disagreement are.*

Each partner listens to the other partner with openness and sympathy, attempting to agree with the dialogue partner as far as is possible while still maintaining integrity with his own tradition. Where he absolutely can agree no further without violating his own integrity, precisely there is the real point of disagreement—which most often turns out to be different from the point of disagreement that was falsely assumed ahead of time.

**SEVENTH COMMANDMENT:** *Dialogue can take place only between equals.*

Participants must come to learn from each other. Therefore, if, for example, the Muslim views Hinduism as inferior, or if the Hindu views

Islam as inferior, there will be no dialogue. If authentic interreligious, interideological dialogue between Muslims and Hindus is to occur, then both the Muslim and the Hindu must come mainly to learn from each other; only then will it be "equal with equal," *"par cum pari"* as Vatican II put it. This rule also indicates that there can be no such thing as a one-way dialogue. For example, Jewish-Christian discussions begun in the 1960s were mainly only prolegomena to interreligious dialogue. Understandably and properly, the Jews came to these exchanges to teach Christians, and the Christians came mainly to learn. But, if authentic interreligious dialogue between Christians and Jews is to occur, then the Jews must also come mainly to learn; only then will it, too, be *par cum pari.*

**EIGHTH COMMANDMENT:** *Dialogue can take place only on the basis of mutual trust.*

Although interreligious, interideological dialogue must occur with some kind of "corporate" dimension, that is, the participants must be involved as members of a religious or ideological community—for instance, as Marxists or Taoists—it is also fundamentally true that only *persons* can enter into dialogue. But a dialogue among persons can be built only on personal trust. Hence it is wise not to tackle the most difficult problems in the beginning, but rather to approach first those issues most likely to provide some common ground, thereby establishing the basis of human trust. Then, gradually, as this personal trust deepens and expands, the more thorny matters can be undertaken. Thus, as in learning we move from the known to the unknown, so in dialogue we proceed from commonly held matters—which, given our mutual ignorance resulting from centuries of hostility, will take us quite some time to discover fully—to discuss matters of disagreement.

**NINTH COMMANDMENT:** *Persons entering into interreligious, interideological dialogue must be at least minimally self-critical of both themselves and their own religious or ideological traditions.*

A lack of such self-criticism implies that one's own tradition already has all the correct answers. Such an attitude makes dialogue not only unnecessary, but even impossible, since we enter into dialogue primarily so we can learn—which obviously is impossible if our tradition has never made a misstep, if it has all the right answers. To be sure, in interreligious, interideological dialogue one must stand within a religious or ideological tradition with integrity and conviction, but such integrity and conviction must include, not exclude, a healthy self-criticism. Without a healthy self-criticism of self and tradition, there can be no dialogue—and, indeed, no integrity.

**TENTH COMMANDMENT:** *Each participant eventually must attempt to experience the partner's religion or ideology "from within."*

A religion or ideology is not merely something of the head, but also of the spirit, heart, and "whole being," individual and communal. John Dunne here speaks of "passing over" into another's religious or ideological experience and then coming back enlightened, broadened, and deepened. While retaining our own religious integrity, we need to find ways of experiencing something of the emotional and spiritual power of the symbols and cultural vehicles of our partner's religion—and then come back to our own enriched and expanded, having experienced at least a little of the affective side of our partner's.

Interreligious, interideological dialogue operates in three areas: the practical, where we collaborate to help humanity; the depth or spiritual dimension where we attempt to experience the partner's religion or ideology "from within"; the cognitive, where we seek understanding and truth. Interreligious, interideological dialogue also has three phases. In the first phase we unlearn misinformation about each other and begin to know each other as we truly are. In phase two we begin to discern values in the partner's tradition and wish to appropriate them into our own tradition. For example, in the Buddhist-Christian dialogue Christians might learn a greater appreciation of the meditative tradition, and Buddhists might learn a greater appreciation of the prophetic, social justice tradition—both values traditionally strongly, though not exclusively, associated with the other's community. If we are serious, persistent, and sensitive enough in the dialogue, we may at times enter into phase three. Here we together begin to explore new areas of reality, of meaning, and of truth, of which neither of us had even been aware before. We are brought face to face with this new, as-yet-unknown-to-us dimension of reality only because of questions, insights, probings produced in the dialogue. We may thus dare to say that patiently pursued dialogue can become an instrument of new "re-velation," a further "un-veiling" of reality—on which we must then act.

There is something radically different about phase one on the one hand and phases two and three on the other. In the latter we do not simply add on quantitatively another "truth" or value from the partner's tradition. Instead, as we assimilate it within our own religious self-understanding, it will proportionately transform our self-understanding. Since our dialogue partner will be in a similar position, we will then be able to witness authentically to those elements of deep value in our own tradition that our partner's tradition may well be able to assimilate with self-transforming profit. All this of course will have to be done with complete integrity on each side, each partner remaining authentically true to the vital core of her own religious tradition. In significant ways, however, that vital core will be perceived and experienced differently under the influence of the dialogue. If the dialogue is carried on with both integrity and openness, the Jew will be even more authentically Jewish and the Christian even more authentically Christian, not from changing the difference in "the other," but because of it. There can be no talk of a syncretism here, for syncretism means amalgamating various elements of different religions into some kind of a (con)fused whole without concern for the integrity of the religions involved—which is not the case with authentic dialogue.

*This "Dialogue Decalogue" was first published in the* Journal of Ecumenical Studies *(Winter, 1983): 1-4, and was slightly revised in 2003 and 2008.*

### Questions for Reflection

1. Why is "dance" an apt metaphor for dialogue? Describe interreligious dialogue as dance.

2. Give examples of dialogue of the head, hands, heart, and wholeness.

3. What suggestions or cautions can you envision for exchange of beliefs and ideas, engaging in joint actions, and sharing prayer or spiritual activities in interreligious contexts?

4. Comment on the ten ground rules for effective interreligious dialogue. Which ones jump out at you as being of particular concern in dialogue events you are planning or participating in? Explain why.

5. Put together your thoughts in response to the following question: Why do I believe that interreligious dialogue is essential today?

### Suggestions for Action

A. What communications skills and listening skills are required for successful dialogue to occur? Which of these do you feel you need to cultivate in preparation for engaging in dialogue?

B. Identify specific ways that each "commandment" of the Dialogue Decalogue can be violated. Act out scenarios that demonstrate one such violation. How might it be addressed in an actual dialogue session?

# DOING EFFECTIVE DIALOGUE— AND LOVING IT

Miriam Therese Winter

The phone rang on New Year's Day. It was Chana calling from Jerusalem, an annual interfaith tradition we have been privileged to carry on for over thirty years. During our lengthy conversation we caught up with the essentials of one another's lives, tapped into the wellspring of one another's spirit, and felt and affirmed yet again the strength of our bond.

Chana and I had met at H.O.P.E. Ecumenical Institute in Jerusalem in 1974 where, for three consecutive summers, we helped facilitate crosscultural and interreligious experiences during a six-week interfaith seminar comprised of Jews, Christians, and Muslims, women and men, conservative and liberal, from local contexts and from abroad. I learned much from her about what it meant to be a Jewish woman in Israel at that time. I learned how to keep a kosher kitchen, what prayers to say at various times, and how it feels to be part of a loving family's Friday evening Shabbat celebration. Because I had experienced these things firsthand, I was able to talk about them afterwards and felt comfortable in Jewish settings. Chana, a Sabra, a native of Israel, also learned something from me, an American and a Christian. In the intervening years, this Jewish scholar has held prominent positions in significant Christian contexts beyond her immediate world. Although we approach things differently, on a level that lies beyond words, we are of one accord. I believe our relationship has helped both of us to bring the fullness of our diversity to a variety of conversation circles in a way that is not divisive. It is at this point of conversation, I am convinced, that real dialogue begins.

## The Context for Doing Dialogue

What is it? Why do it? Why is it so difficult? How do we begin? How can we make it work? The following pages will address the questions that accompany a decision to dialogue, making specific application to dialogue that is interreligious or interfaith.

Interreligious or interfaith dialogue, at the periphery for decades, has surfaced once again in religious life and in the academy. Today, having achieved widespread relevance and a sense of urgency, it is at the very top of our proposed agendas. Most people are aware we live in a world of difference. This different world is no longer "over there" but in our neighborhoods and often in our living rooms. Our global society is irrevocably linked by networks of communication and economic realities. In an age of instant messaging, distance is irrelevant. Suddenly, everything is right here. Just as swiftly, we are out there confronted by the unfamiliar, catapulted into crosscultural situations our ancestors could never have imagined. This shift in relationship between here and there has brought us to the tipping point. We seem more willing now to face our differences rather than obliterate them, more inclined to seek an understanding beneficial to all.

The "other," the unfamiliar person, lives next door, has married one of our children, is essential to our workforce, and has become an integral part of our American way of life. As a nation of both immigrant and indigenous diversity, we are accustomed to the stranger. What is happening today, however, is different. Previous to this historical moment, those who came to America in order to start a new life left one world for another. Today a vast number of worlds are colliding in our midst, buttressed by media images indicating how, for better or for worse, our nation is inseparably joined to other nations an ocean or more away. The jobs that used to support our families now belong to people on the other side of the planet. So much of what we use and own—the food we eat, the clothes we wear, our electronic equipment, our cars, and the fuel to meet our insatiable energy needs–has come from somewhere else, while citizens in diaspora are establishing an American presence all around the world.

An emerging global society profoundly impacts the way we live our lives, challenging our basic premises, predicting a future radically different from the social/political landscape reminiscent of the way we were. We are in the midst of a paradigm shift that is reshaping us at every level as a new and far more integrated world, slowly, but ever so surely, and more than a little chaotically, struggles to come to birth. At the same time terror, misrepresentation, and prejudicial misunderstanding have infiltrated society, causing friction and fragmentation to obstruct commonsense efforts toward harmony and peace. In such a world dialogue is fundamental to survival and to systemic change. Like all those things that contribute to the well-being of a people, the ability to converse with respect is essential not only to our nation's security but also to our everyday life. For this reason scholars' efforts to initiate sustainable dialogue must spill over into the streets.

Interreligious or interfaith dialogue means an intentional engagement with those whose religion or faith tradition differs from our own. Such dialogue can take a variety of forms: discussion or debate on significant issues or subjects of mutual concern; a presentation on a selected theme, followed by a response; a structured conversation. Since this sounds like something we do all the time, why is it so difficult?

Interfaith dialogue is challenging for a variety of reasons. Being comfortable with that which we do not know is not a disposition that everyone can claim. Although we live in a country that is eclectically multicultural, many people have difficulty making room in their lives or in their hearts for that which is utterly different. The familiar is our security in a rapidly changing world that is pushing to the limit our capacity to adapt. A focus on family and personal growth and on succeeding in a competitive world leaves little time or energy to strike up a conversation when there seems to be no common ground. People are often too tired or too stressed to do the preparation necessary to understand and appreciate that which on the surface appears to have nothing to do with them. The white picket fence may stand beside the stark façade of a condo, but the boundary line prevails, creating a chasm far too wide for the timid to step across.

Not knowing what to do or say and being unwilling to listen and learn is a barrier to dialogue. So is thinking we know all there is to know or all that is necessary for us to know. Having fixed assumptions that define and delineate "us" and "them" also inhibits dialogue and labels some as enemies who might otherwise be our friends. A lingering dislike of foreigners and a propensity for retaliation characteristic of our turbulent times stifle that which is conducive to a rational exchange of views. It is especially hard to initiate dialogue when either misinformation or representative data distorted by ignorance or fear is so predominant.

Dialogue along less conventional lines is always difficult. Religious dialogue is even more difficult, which should come as no surprise. If this is the case among members of the same faith tradition, and it often is, imagine the complexity of dialogue across faith traditions, where the challenge of comprehending divergent creeds, codes, customs, and their corresponding theologies seems an insurmountable task. When confronted by diverse understandings of God, the average individual assumes we are talking about different gods. It might seem best, therefore, to leave this kind of conversation to those whose vocation and vocabulary reflect the prerequisite skills needed for a favorable outcome. That attitude is precisely what we want to overturn. Interreligious dialogue is not only for the elite. Our ultimate goal is that one day it will be commonplace.

Once we are convinced of the value and necessity of interreligious dialogue at any time and in any place, we face some challenging questions. Where do we begin? What will it take to be successful? What follows is a perspective that arises from my experience, one view among many in a wide open field that traverses multiple disciplines.

## Models and Means

Dialogue happens when we talk to one another in an interchange of information and ideas that fosters mutual understanding. A spontaneous and frank conversation, an energetic debate, a collective response to a formal and informative presentation are opportunities for considering how others see the world and how rich is the diversity within it. An enlightening exchange or a constructive give-and-take may not always happen because of the limitations of either the model or the means. Yet even in the absence of achieving a goal of significant interfaith understanding, the effort itself will prepare the way for a more fruitful and satisfying outcome sometime later on. Speech is prevalent in dialogical endeavors, yet talk is not the only way, nor is it always the most effective way of interfaith communication. Interfaith dialogue can and does occur in the interstices of silence, when a level of trust releases the heart from protective custody, and the spirit of each becomes the spirit of all through an encounter with the Divine. Deep dialogue such as this communicates in a language beyond words to those who have learned how to listen and have prepared themselves to hear. An open forum is not the place for deep dialogue to occur. It requires a more intimate setting and a spirit of hospitality that makes everyone feel at home.

Here then are some examples of models and the means for doing effective dialogue:

### Conversation Circles

When we introduced a required course titled "Dialogue in a World of Difference" into our seminary's core curriculum, there was some concern that it might not work, but I was convinced it would. We were in my comfort zone, which is the unpredictable, and I would be teaching the course. When I step out into the unknown, I expect to be led by the Spirit to accomplish the task at hand. Trust in the Spirit is prerequisite to interfaith dialogue, for it is God's work we are undertaking in building a more unified world.

The structure of the course was nontraditional, and it would be team-taught. Anyone in academia knows that if you put three professors in a room you will get four very different opinions about how to proceed. But this was not the case. The three members of our team, diverse in gender, age, nationality, religious affiliation, and academic disciplines, were not only colleagues but also friends who work well together as individuals and as a team. We also have significant experience in crosscultural and inter-faith settings. The course itself modeled difference in a variety of ways: in the syllabus, readings, and assignments; in the content, the process, and the overall dynamics; as well as in its participants, among whom there was diversity in culture, nationality, race, gender, age, orientation, educational background, vocational call, professional career, marital status, and family life. There was also diversity of faith among students with a religious affiliation and among those without one. The backstory to "Dialogue in a World of Difference" could well be described as difference in a world of dialogue. Convening a richly diverse group and setting an appropriate context were essential preparations. Effective interfaith dialogue requires doing some work in advance.

In an academic context some might say that the first three sessions of the course were a waste of time, but they were the core foundation that we would subsequently build upon.

Session one: "Let me tell you who I am." We got to know one another by sharing our personal stories and in the process set the framework for building community.

Session two: "Let me tell you about my religion and the context of my faith." We shared basic information about our religion, faith, spirituality, and what these mean to us. Images or names of God were only briefly introduced in the time available.

Session three: "Let me tell you about my culture and about my country." This gave international students a chance to talk about home and family, about favorite foods and customs, and to explore those things about life in America that they did not understand. It was also an introduction to the political context of the countries represented by the class.

The following quote from Margaret Wheatley's *Turning to One Another* articulates the underlying ethos of our opening design:

> I believe we can change the world
> if we start listening to one another again.
> Simple, honest, human conversation.
> Not mediation, negotiation, problem-solving,

debate, or public meetings.
Simple, truthful conversation
where we each have a chance to speak,
we each feel heard, and we each listen well.[1]

The next three sessions, each with formal presentations by faculty in the field, focused on a theoretical approach to "Sharing Our Sacred Scriptures," "Theological and Ethical Frameworks," and "Spirituality, Ritual, Prayer." The three sessions that followed put theory into practice: "Peace and Reconciliation," which included time for those caught up in the dynamics of war and peace to vocalize their concerns, "A Taste of Ramadan," and "Praying Together." Because it was the month of Ramadan, the class took an off-campus trip to a public *Iftar* for the breaking of the Muslim fast, then wrote a brief reflection on their crosscultural experience, focusing on what they had learned. The final session consisted of a meal at the home of our Muslim professor, a celebratory and fitting way to bring closure to the class.

The classic approach to interfaith dialogue is to start right out with the hard questions, allowing proponents of opposing views to make their positions known. The ensuing dialogue is in response to those positions. In our class we did not avoid the issues. We simply delayed addressing them until a more propitious time. Laying the groundwork by listening to and getting to know one another made it easier to empathize with those who spoke with passion about some concern and to hear better what they had to say when it came time to do so. It was amazing to see the class evolve. Individuals reached a level of togetherness that exceeded what ordinarily occurs in seminary settings, especially when subgroups sprawled around the room were deep into some kind of sharing. There was genuine regret when the course was over. Relationships had been established, along with a level of trust that implied the conversation could continue into the future should the occasion arise.

In our team evaluation, it was clear to us that our goals had been met. Through our facilitation, the course had 1) fostered an understanding of one another through information sharing and community-building action; 2) provided opportunities for developing listening and communication skills in multicultural contexts; and 3) offered a context for wrestling with the challenging questions and issues of our times and for discussing potentially divisive issues constructively and without animosity. Projected outcomes also had been achieved. Students had 1) a sense of collegiality and community across religious, cultural, and gender lines; 2) a rudimentary understanding of crosscultural and interfaith dialogue and the ability to participate meaningfully in multicultural conversations; and 3) an ability to integrate and apply their learnings to the task at hand. The successful completion of action tasks assigned during the class demonstrated this last outcome.

Several other factors contributed to the successful outcome of this interfaith dialogue experience. We were seated in a circle. Facing one another made conversation easier, evoking a sense of togetherness before it had been achieved. The circular model emphasized that all who were present were equal and had equal opportunity both to contribute to and to receive from what was to be learned. Even those less inclined to speak participated fully, for facilitators were sensitive to the fact that introverts need more time to think and factored that into the process. The circle and the process ensured that no one voice would dominate, no position seize control. The sessions opened and closed with a brief, centering ritual, more often than not a silent prayer inclusive of everyone.

An effective teaching model is one where the content and its delivery are pedagogically integral. This means that the faculty members had to adjust to the model in order for the outcomes and goals to be achieved. The students had to see in us what was to be accomplished. Diverse approaches were welcome as reflected in the different styles of leadership shared. The three of us enjoyed the experience of both learning and teaching, were at ease with the informality, and did not have a need to be in control of the outcome. To walk the talk is critical in interfaith dialogue, for this demonstrates that it works. To witness what one values validates for others the principle and the importance of practicing what we preach.

*Wisdom Circles*

The interfaith wisdom circles of the Women's Leadership Institute that I began a decade ago are current models that give credibility to the substance of this essay. In this program in applied spirituality, relationships happen effortlessly and deep dialogue flourishes. One woman put it this way: "It was awesome to experience the Spirit of God with six women who had six different beliefs about God." Here is another's response: "So many of us have, for a long time, had the desire to rise above our limited areas of explored faith. I got the feeling that together we could fly. I so much appreciate the fact that I am spending Shabbat in a holy place." From larger and smaller wisdom circles, authentic dialogue spirals out into a vast web of innerconnectedness formed by past participants and their associates.

During this nine-month adventure in doing interfaith dialogue, participants experience an awakening to a new way of being in the world and to our inherent oneness. Christians, Muslims, Jews, and women from other faith traditions and with no particular faith affiliation listen intently to one another and affirm a shared sisterhood. Together we do theology, encourage creativity, design and celebrate ritual, integrate theory and its application, share an immersion experience by entering into dialogue with a sister circle of incarcerated women, and, through the design and implementation of a project in leadership, hone our ability to replicate what we have learned by extending it beyond our circle. We also eat together often, for a shared spirit is often made manifest in a common meal. Our prayer is expressed through metaphors such as light, water, fire, stars, and themes that weave through our everyday lives as reflected in symbol and song. This model is rooted in a feminist perspective that is based on justice, globally oriented, attentive to diversity, and ritually expressed. It is a vehicle for transformative change in religion and society.

## Concluding Recommendations

Here are some suggestions for initiating authentic interreligious dialogue. While the value of a well-designed one-time event ought not be underestimated, these recommendations presume that interaction will continue beyond an initial encounter.

Be clear with each undertaking why you want to do interreligious dialogue and what you hope to accomplish. Make the outcomes concrete, and set realistic goals.

Shift your focus from dialogue to establishing a relationship. As the relationship is being formed, dialogue will occur. Once there is mutual trust and a bond that seems relatively secure, politically and theologically sensitive issues can be discussed more fruitfully.

Let dialogue be the byproduct of collaborative action. Identify those with whom you would like to communicate, then do something together. Share a meal. Implement a project. Undertake a service-oriented task to benefit someone in need. Visit one another's sacred sites. Carry out a mutual crosscultural immersion experience, then share with each other what that was like and how you felt about it. Clarify misunderstandings. Respond to lingering questions. Inherent here is the principle that actions speak louder than words, yet words are helpful and even necessary for some actions to be understood.

Above all, learn how to listen. Learn how to hear what is really being said even when the words get in the way and trigger a reaction. Try to imagine what the world is like from the other person's point of view.

Be alert to the complexity of diversity. Even among people who look alike, no two are the same. Tough questions often arise from differences that are seldom seen or too threatening to talk about. Sometimes authentic dialogue is easier with those whose religion or culture differs from our own.

Be sensitive to the issue of critical mass. Interreligious dialogue is more likely to be authentic when there is more than a token presence—ideally, a balanced representation.

Reflect upon broader outcomes, which call for long-range goals. Shared spirit, common cause, a world united on issues of justice and committed to living in peace can come about through dialogue, one achievable goal at a time. Being together, working together, and in whatever way possible, praying together with those whose culture or faith tradition are different from our own have immense value and give flesh to the vision of hope that surely is of God.

A final recommendation: Stop talking about dialogue and just do it. Before long you will find that you, too, are loving it.

**Note**

1. Margaret J. Wheatley, *Turning to One Another: Simple Conversations to Restore Hope to the Future* (San Francisco, CA: Berrett-Koehler, 2002), p. 3.

**Questions for Reflection**

1. How important is it for members of one religion to feel comfortable in the setting of another religion? How can interreligious engagement serve this end?

2. The author suggests shifting emphasis from dialogue to building relationships. How could we fashion dialogue events that would foster creating friendships? Should this be an implicit or explicit goal of dialogue?

3. What factors affect how we do interreligious dialogue today? (For instance, how do we do interreligious dialogue when "the other" lives next door or is married to our cousin? How do we do dialogue when so many people are only marginally involved in their own tradition?)

4. The author is comfortable with entering into an unfamiliar world, confident that the spirit will provide guidance. Have you found this to be true when people from diverse backgrounds come together dedicated to mutual listening and learning? Do you agree with her advice: "Just do it"?

5.   Is the three-step series of questions the author used in her "conversation circles" applicable to interreligious dialogue sessions in general? Why or why not?

6.   Is it better to delay hard questions until some sense of community has been established within a group?

7.   An effective teaching model integrates what is taught with how it is taught. How can this principle be applied to interreligious dialogue?

8.   What possible collaborative actions might accompany interreligious dialogue?

**Suggestions for Action**

A.   Reflect on your story, your experience of faith, your religion, and your cultural background. What would you want others to know about you in an interreligious context?

B.   Begin formulating questions that you have regarding members of other religions and their experience.

C.   Design a "conversation circle" as described by the author.

# Storytelling as a Key Methodology for Interfaith Youth Work

Eboo Patel, April Kunze, and Noah Silverman

*I can only answer the question "What am I to do?" if I can answer the prior question "Of what story or stories do I find myself a part?"*

—Alasdair MacIntyre

## Introduction: Storytelling

In the spring of 2003, a diverse group of high school students assembled on the stage of a Chicago exhibition hall to perform a spoken-word piece titled "The Sacred Stories Project." The stories that formed the piece were exercises in representing the importance of the central value of hospitality in Judaism, Christianity, and Islam. The stories were written and performed by members of the Interfaith Youth Core's Chicago Youth Council, a group of Jewish, Christian, and Muslim teenagers who met regularly to volunteer across the city and to discuss how their various religious traditions inspire them to work for a better world. Each story was a young person's interpretation of how an ancient religious narrative or practice exemplifying hospitality should be applied in the contemporary world. The stories were richly textured and complex, but their key message was clear: We have to take care of each other. This command is in all our religions, and following its imperative is our only chance for survival as a human race.

The process of writing their stories, coupled with performing them in juxtaposition to each other, caused the members of the Chicago Youth Council to realize that, while their diverse traditions all called them to the same value, they each did so in their own language. The Jewish stories were different from the Christian stories, which were different from the

Muslim stories. As one Jewish participant articulated, "I came to realize, perhaps for the first time, that my story was distinctly a Jewish story and that my inspiration to serve others, while universal, was colored in distinctly Jewish ways." The participants all agreed that the experience of service, storytelling, and dialogue had not only increased their understanding of each others' traditions, but also strengthened their sense of belonging, inheritance, and identity within their own respective traditions.

At its heart, interfaith dialogue is about identity—one's own identity and the identities of the other participants. Identity, both individual and communal, constructs itself through stories and storytelling. It is through the act of telling personal narratives—and the involved processes of reflecting on, distilling, and constructing our "life story"—that we come to form an idea of who we are. Duke University theologian Stanley Hauerwas, who has written extensively on the centrality of stories to Christian theology and human identity, explains the role of narrative in identity as follows:

> Narrative plays a larger part in our lives than we often imagine. For example, we frequently introduce ourselves through narrative. To be sure, any story with which we identify "ourselves" can be and should be constantly tested by the history we have lived. But the telling of the narrative is itself a reinterpretation of the history. We see that because the self is historically formed we require a narrative to speak about it if we are to speak at all. One should not think of oneself as exemplifying or being some individual instance of a self, but one understands in what his or her selfhood consists only insofar as he or she learns to tell that particular story.[1]

This remarkable phenomenon—the generative power of personal narratives in identity-formation—is now being verified by recent scientific research. As noted in a recent *New York Times* article, "We are [all] continually updating a [screenplay] of our own life—and the way in which we visualize each scene not only shapes how we think about ourselves, but how we behave, new studies find." Dan P. McAdams, a professor of psychology at Northwestern, is quoted as saying, "We find that these [personal] narratives guide behavior in every moment, and frame not only how we see the past but how we see ourselves in the future." It turns out, perhaps not surprisingly, that the brain is naturally hardwired for narrative construction. Summarizing the new research, the article concludes, "The point is that the narrative themes are, as much as any other trait, driving factors in people's behavior, the researchers say. Seeing oneself as acting in a movie or a play is not merely fantasy or indulgence; it is fundamental to how people work out who it is they are, and may become."[2]

In some ways, this research merely constitutes a scientific corollary to what religious communities have known throughout history: stories have an awesome power over the human imagination. "Stories are not substitute explanations we can someday hope to supplant with more straightforward accounts," writes Hauerwas. "Precisely to the contrary, narratives are necessary to our understanding of those aspects of our existence which admit no further explanation—i.e., God, the world, and the self."[3] Not only is storytelling generative of individual identity, but it also builds communal identity. All of the world's traditions, cultures, and nations—including intensely secular ones—employ stories to create and sustain their communities' identity: stories of creation, of the prophets and founding fathers, of where we have come, and ultimately, of where we hope to go. Coming out of the Christian tradition, Hauerwas goes so far as to define community as the end result of a process that begins with stories: "Christian convictions take the form of a story, or perhaps better, a set of stories that constitutes a tradition, which in turn creates and forms a community."[4]

Hauerwas argues that even the relationship between self and community can be understood only through narrative:

> Narrative is the characteristic form of our awareness of ourselves as *historical* beings who must give an account of the purposive relation between temporally discrete realities. Indeed, the ability to provide such an account, to sustain its growth in a living tradition, is the central criterion for identifying a group of people as a community. Community joins us with others to further the growth of a tradition whose manifold storylines are meant to help individuals identify and navigate the path to the good. The self is subordinate to the community rather than vice versa, for we discover the self through a community's narrated tradition.[5]

For Hauerwas, narrative is instrumental not only in constructing one's own, individual identity, but also in locating that identity within the tradition of a larger community. As the members of the Chicago Youth Council discovered through the "Sacred Stories Project," each of our stories is one thread intrinsically interwoven into the larger story of our tradition, the "rope" that binds us into community.

## Young People and the "Faith Line"

Because an intricate relationship exists between personal narrative and a "community's narrated tradition," storytelling is a key methodology for interfaith youth work. For one thing, it helps young people strengthen their own identity within and sense of belonging to their community's tradition. It also enables the creation of a larger identity that supersedes individual and communal identity. One's own identity and the identities of the other participants may form the fabric of an interfaith dialogue, but the ultimate goal of interfaith work is the creation of a larger identity that makes room for the distinctiveness of different traditions while encompassing them around their shared, universal values. This larger identity is called pluralism: the conviction that people believing in different creeds and belonging to different communities need to learn to live together in what the theologian Wilfred Cantwell Smith called "mutual trust and mutual loyalty."[6] Those who share this conviction are pluralists, and they come from every religious and political creed on the planet, for pluralism is neither syncretism nor relativism. It is a form of proactive cooperation that affirms the identity of the constituent communities while emphasizing that the well-being of each and all depends on the health of the whole.

Though anyone, by definition, can be a pluralist without sacrificing any of his or her individual or communal identity, sadly not everyone is, and the twenty-first century has already come to be dominated by a tremendous ideological divide between pluralists and those opposed to pluralism: totalitarians. Where pluralists respect the religious identity of others, totalitarians seek to blot out any identity but their own. Where pluralists seek relationships across religious divides that provide for mutual inspiration and growth, totalitarians seek to cow, condemn, or—at the extreme—kill anyone not like themselves. Where pluralists seek to work with others for the common good, totalitarians seek to destroy the dream of a common life together. The one characteristic they do have in common is that either one can come from any religious and political creed. Rabbi Abraham Joshua Heschel was a Jewish pluralist; Rabbi Meir Kahane was a Jewish totalitarian. The Rev. Dr. Martin Luther King, Jr., was a Christian pluralist; Eric Rudolph is a Christian totalitarian. Imam Feisal Abdul Rauf is a Muslim pluralist; Osama bin Laden is a Muslim totalitarian.

Thus the central challenge of our time is indeed the faith line, but it does not exist, as some have argued, where religious civilizations bump up against each other but, rather, within and across all of them. As Martha Nussbaum writes, "The real clash is not a civilizational one between 'Islam' and 'the West,' but instead a clash within virtually all modern nations—between people who are prepared to live with others who are different, on terms of equal respect, and those who seek the protection of homogeneity, achieved through the domination of a single religious or ethnic tradition."[7] What is perhaps most intriguing about the faith line—

this struggle between pluralists and totalitarians—is that the majority of people in the world are standing right on it, uncertain and undecided about their allegiance. They most likely incline toward pluralism and away from totalitarianism. In many ways, they are waiting to be won over by one side or the other, and the recruitment strategies of both sides take the form of storytelling.

As multiple scholars from multiple fields—Benjamin Barber, Mark Jeurgensmeyer, Bruce Lawrence, Jessica Stern, to name a few—have demonstrated, religious totalitarianism relies on convincing young recruits that their terrorist exploits will return their community to a fictional past when the community was pure, followed God's path, and received God's glory without complication. This meta-narrative transcends religious totalitarian movements, but one can see how stories are used more directly to recruit young people to adopt a totalitarian outlook. In 2001, bin Laden released a statement to Al Jazeera that provides a quintessential example of how totalitarians employ stories to engage young people in religious violence. In it, he tells the story of a boy who discovers that an animal (America) is blocking a monk's path (the Muslim world). The boy slaughters the animal, to which the monk responds, "My son, today you are better than me." Bin Laden then comments on the story (emphasis added):

> God Almighty lit up this boy's heart with the light of faith, and he began to make sacrifices for the sake of "There is no god but God." *This is a unique and valuable story which the youth of Islam are waiting for their scholars to tell them*, which would show the youth that these [the 9/11 hijackers] are the people who have given up everything for the sake of "There is no god but God."[8]

Bin Laden follows this story with another, this one about how the Prophet's uncle, Hamza bin Abd al-Muttalib, killed an unjust man. In this way he draws a connection and authority from the time of the Prophet, from a historical figure that Muslims consider a hero, and claims that this man's heroism came from his violence. "He won a great victory," bin Laden says of al-Muttalib, "God Almighty raised him up to the status of lord of the martyrs."[9] Through both allegorical storytelling and religious narratives, bin Laden conveys his point to young Muslims compellingly: In order to intertwine your story fully and faithfully into the story of Islam, you must engage in violence against those who are unjust and stand in our way (in this case, the U.S. and its allies).

Religious pluralists have, throughout history, employed narrative to attract young people to their vision as well. King, one of the most visionary pluralists of modern times, was a master storyteller, and he too spoke in both allegory and religious narratives. One such instance was his prophetic "I Have Been to the Mountaintop" sermon, delivered immediately before his assassination. Drawing from the story of Moses in the Hebrew Bible/ Scripture, King told his followers that, while he might not get there with them, he has "seen the promised land" of racial justice and equality. In this one sermon, King managed to recount both a biblical narrative of justice and redemption while simultaneously weaving in and retelling the story of the civil rights movement.

Aside from content and purpose, where the recruitment strategies of totalitarians and pluralists diverge is in their target audience. Totalitarians are after young people, and they have been remarkably successful at recruiting them. One of the saddest and most alarming trends of the religious violence gripping the world today is that the ages of the people doing most of the fighting, killing, and dying are generally between fifteen and thirty. This alarming truth is only partially explained by the fact that the populations of the most religiously volatile areas of the world are stunningly young: Seventy-five percent of India's billion-plus citizens are not yet twenty-five; eighty-five percent of the people who live in the Palestinian territories are under the age of thirty-three; more than two-thirds of Iranians are younger than thirty; the median age in Iraq is nineteen-and-a-half.

Though these demographics certainly make the phenomenon of youth involvement in religious violence more likely, they do not tell the full story. In a world divided by the faith line, we must come to terms with the fact that it is the religious totalitarians who have best succeeded at tapping into the passions of young people and forging their identities. Young people have always been instrumental to the success of social movements, from the U.S. civil rights movement to the Hitler youth. On the side of pluralism, many of its greatest leaders were themselves young when they assumed their leadership positions. King was only twenty-six when he led the Montgomery bus boycott. Gandhi was even younger when he began organizing for South Asian civil rights in early-twentieth-century South Africa. His Holiness the Dalai Lama was younger still, just eighteen years old, when he led his government into exile in India and began his campaign for a free Tibet.

Today, however, religious pluralists can and need to do a better job of directing their stories at young people. Youth programs now are often the top item in a congregation's or interfaith organization's newsletter but the last line in the budget. If religious pluralism has a chance of overcoming totalitarianism in the century ahead, this situation has to change. Young people must reassume their position as the heroes, leaders, and practitioners of religious pluralism. It was in recognition of this dire situation that a group of religiously diverse young people founded the Interfaith Youth Core (IFYC) in 1998. From its outset, the IFYC has been dedicated to the mission of empowering religiously diverse young people to build pluralism, and, from the beginning, it was clear that one of the best ways to accomplish that was through storytelling.

## The Interfaith Youth Core's Storytelling Methodology

The IFYC has discovered that, especially when working with young people, stories are a matchless tool for interfaith sharing and thus understanding. Storytelling provides a bridge for overcoming some of the major obstacles frequently encountered in interfaith dialogue by opening the possibility for a different kind of conversation. One must recognize that, as members of religious communities that have historically clashed on theological or political issues, we are often inculcated to view others through the narrow lens of how and where our communities disagree. Often, this indoctrination becomes so pervasive that we believe the only conversation of faith we can have with our religious "others" is about our "otherness." We can, however, have another conversation. Instead of focusing on the myriad differences and political struggles among traditions, we can encourage the participants to identify and to examine their multiple shared values through personal storytelling.

Personal storytelling moves the encounter from competing notions of "Truth" to varied human experiences of life, which possess the unique quality of being both infinite and common. Who does not know pain and loss? Who does not know love and togetherness? What young person does not know the pressure to meet parents' expectations or to care for a family in their absence? In all IFYC dialogue curricula the questions always start with, "Tell a story of a time when—." Participants are then called to relate stories from their experience and their tradition that speak to the shared value at hand, be it service, hospitality, stewardship of creation, teaching, caring for the sick and elderly, etc. The combination of shared values and storytelling thus allows for what the IFYC calls a "dialogue of life." Young people in IFYC programs spend their time talking about what it is like to be a young person of a particular identity growing up in a diverse world. They make connections between challenges they have in common—such as modesty, dating, dietary restrictions, and observance of holidays—and they share how they address those challenges in keeping with the unique traditions of their specific religious or moral community.

More importantly, they make connections between their shared values— fighting racism and bigotry, eradicating poverty, caring for creation—and they share how their tradition has instilled those values in them.

The IFCY storytelling methodology thus differs significantly from two other modes of dialogue that are prominent in the interfaith field: dialogues of theology—where a priest, minister, rabbi, imam, and swami discuss the nature of the divine—and dialogues of politics—where Jews and Muslims discuss Israel/Palestine or Buddhists and Hindus discuss Sri Lanka. These two modes of dialogue are useful and necessary in the broader field, but the IFYC believes more productive conversations occur among people who already possess pluralist relationships with each other. The goal of the storytelling methodology is to build those sorts of pluralist relationships among young people.

Part of the power of the storytelling methodology is that it empowers young people to be teachers and social contributors. When a young person is asked to tell a story from his or her experience, the act inherently promotes the value of that person's experience to something capable of enriching others. In asking the question, a facilitator is in essence saying, "Your life is so rich and interesting that everyone else around the room will benefit simply by hearing you retell it." This youth empowerment promotes young people to be what the IFYC calls "scholars of their own experience."[10] When young people approach IFYC staff with the excuse that they cannot participate in our dialogues because they have not memorized the Qur'ān, or did not pay attention in Sunday school, or never learned Hebrew, the response is simply that it does not matter. Young people in this methodology are not required to be scholars of their traditions; they speak from their own life experience of which they are the world's foremost experts. The line repeatedly is, "No one in the world knows what it is like to be you better than you. Please tell us a story that will teach us a piece of what that has meant."

As participants become more familiar with the methodology, their storytelling evolves, from stories that are exclusively experiential—"this is my experience of living out this shared value"—to stories that become more theologically grounded—"it is the teaching of [for example: *tikun olam*/Matthew 25/the Hadith of Mercy] that inspires me to live this out." Good facilitators of this methodology are able to help young people move along this spectrum, helping them to see the role their tradition played in making a given value a part of their life. Excellent facilitators and inter-faith organizers also possess the ability to tell grander, master narratives that intertwine their personal story and the story of their tradition in such a way that it points toward pluralism. One excellent example of such a master narrative comes from Jenan, a Muslim member of the IFYC staff:

> My mother is a devout Muslim. My mother's best friend, Aunty Diana, is a devout Catholic. I spent most of my childhood growing up in the Middle Eastern country of Qatar. Throughout our years in Qatar, Aunty Diana and her family were closer to us than our extended family. Religious holidays were the best time of year, when anonymous presents would magically appear on our doorstep on Christmas morning and on Eid we would have a house full of friends from various faith communities (Christian, Sikh, Hindu, etc.) celebrating with us. Aunty Diana, however, was a much more intricate part of our lives. When I was fourteen, my parents performed the pilgrimage of *hajj,* and, upon their return, my mother began wearing *hijab.* I, however, had started to grow away from Islam and could not understand my mother's emerging religious identity. During this time, it was Aunty Diana who would often negotiate and attempt to bridge the growing gap between my mother and me. My family later relocated to Chicago and after a few years, I stumbled upon the path of rediscovering my own religious identity as a Muslim. I started praying, fasting, engaging in community service, and I too decided to wear *hijab.*
>
> Two years ago we were reunited with Aunty Diana for a brief period of time. She visited us and stayed with us in our home. I drove her to church every Sunday, and she woke me when she noticed that I had missed my alarm for *Fajr* (dawn) prayer. The relationship that exists between her and my family reminds me of the story of Jafar-et-Tayyara, who was a cousin and close companion of the Prophet Muhammad. During the years of persecution from Mecca, Jafar was given the responsibility of leading a group of Muslims to take refuge in the Christian Kingdom of Abyssinia (Ethiopia). Upon hearing of their arrival, King Negus called Jafar into his court. He asked him to speak of Muhammad, and to read from the Qur'ān. Jafar conveyed the message of Muhammad to King Negus and then recited the verses about the story of Jesus and his mother, Mary. Upon hearing this, Negus welcomed the Muslim refugee community into his kingdom and encouraged them to practice Islam freely. The Christian community protected their new neighbors, and each community took care of the other while respecting their dignity and distinctiveness. Such is the relationship between my family and Aunty Diana. While we are all devout in our respective religious traditions, what brings us together is our own faith journeys, which we have struggled in and experienced side by side. Like Jafar and Negus, the strength of our friendship lies in the values we share and our individual relationship with the divine.

Not only does Jenan's story relate the personal experience of her family to a story strongly rooted in her tradition, but it also makes the point that

Islam has a strong basis for supporting pluralist relationships, as illustrated by the relationship between Jafar and Negus and their respective communities. These types of stories, while beyond what can be expected from first-time participants in dialogue, are necessary to continue the tradition of inspiring and recruiting young people to the side of pluralism.

## Conclusion

The great rabbi, Abraham Joshua Heschel, once said, "First we begin in sound and then we must move to deed." Stories are just the beginning. They provide a powerful call to action, to a better self, for each of us individually, for our religious communities, for our nation, and for our world. However, without action their full potential for social change remains unrealized. A crucial component to the storytelling methodology outlined above is social action through the form of service-learning. Each storytelling dialogue is coupled with an opportunity for the participants to leave the dialogue circle, go out into their communities, and embody the stories of service and compassion they have told. When individual youth hear stories from others that resonate with their own experience, they can be transformed. When young people from different backgrounds join forces to combat social ills, society can be transformed. The greatest story that all our traditions tell is one of a community committed to the betterment of the world. Interfaith youth work, through storytelling and service-learning, can write the next chapter of that story.

### Notes

1. Stanley Hauerwas, *The Peaceable Kingdom: A Primer in Christian Ethics* (Notre Dame, IN: University of Notre Dame Press, 1983), p. 26.

2. Benedict Carey, "This Is Your Life (and How You Tell It)," *New York Times*, May 22, 2007, Health section, Online edition.

3. Hauerwas, *The Peaceable Kingdom*, p. 26.

4. Hauerwas, *The Peaceable Kingdom*, p. 24.

5. Hauerwas, *The Peaceable Kingdom*, p. 28.

6. Wilfred Cantwell Smith, *The Faith of Other Men* (New York: Harper & Row Publishers, 1962), p. 13.

7. Martha Nussbaum, *The Clash Within: Democracy, Religious Violence, and India's Future* (Cambridge, MA: The Belknap Press of Harvard University Press, 2007).

8. Bruce Lawrence, *Messages to the World: The Statements of Osama bin Laden* (London: Verso, 2005), p. 154.

9. Eboo Patel, *Acts of Faith: The Story of an American Muslim—The Struggle for the Soul of a Generation* (Boston, MA: Beacon Press, 2007), pp. 130–131.

10. Eboo Patel and Mariah Neuroth, "The Interfaith Youth Core: Building Chicago as a Model Interfaith Youth City," in Eboo Patel and Patrice Brodeur, eds., *Building the Interfaith Youth Movement: Beyond Dialogue to Action* (Lanham, MD: Rowman & Littlefield Publishers, 2006), p. 172.

.

## Questions for Reflection

1. Take a moment to think about a story that expresses what your faith means to you. Tell your story to others, and hear their stories as well. Share your observations about these stories.

2. What are some ways that storytelling can be incorporated into interreligious dialogue? Is storytelling uniquely suited to dialogue? If so, why?

3. Do you find that Jews, Christians, and Muslims tend to tell distinctly different stories? Explain.

4. We can disagree about dogmas. Can we disagree about stories? In what ways are Jewish, Christian, and Muslim stories different from Jewish, Christian, and Muslim teachings?

5. Can young people's engagement in interreligious dialogue strengthen their identity in their own faith tradition? How might that work?

6. How should interreligious dialogue differ when engaged in by different age groups: teens, young adults, older adults?

7. The authors claim that pluralism is neither syncretism nor relativism, and its opposite is totalitarianism. What do they mean? What is pluralism? Do you agree that pluralism is the only viable stance that religious people can take today?

8. According to the authors, the easy part of dialogue is exploring one religion over against another. The real challenge is within and across religious lines, between pluralists and totalitarians. What implications does this hold for the goals and practice of interreligious dialogue?

9. Many young people are teetering between pluralism and totalitarianism. Name stories from your religious tradition that could inspire young people to adopt a pluralist perspective. What obstacles exist in working with young people around religious matters?

10. The IFYC uses storytelling to engage young people in a "dialogue

about life." How can this model be applied to interreligious dialogue? Should dialogue about religion be set aside in favor of dialogue about life?

11. Give examples of how personal narratives might be related to master narratives—that is, personal stories intertwined with stories from the tradition.

**Suggestions for Action**

A.   Identify approaches to interreligious dialogue that would be effective with young people.

B.   Name characteristics and give examples of pluralism versus totalitarianism.

C.   If you haven't done so already, tell a story that has been transformative in your life.

D.   Create a dialogue program for young people from different faith traditions.

# 4

# THE NEXT THING TO DIALOGUE

Edith Howe and S. Mark Heim[1]

A line often attributed to the poet W. H. Auden says that love, like sleep, resists approaches that are too intense. All of us understand what is meant. There are things that in their very nature must be sought by a kind of indirection. There are things that can only be seen if you are not looking directly at them. Friendship generally arises among those enjoying time together intently occupied otherwise than in planning how to get to know each other. The young sports fan learns math in the process of figuring batting averages.

This pattern is especially characteristic of certain kinds of learning. It is not only that they may happen so. It is that they happen best and most regularly in that manner. So it is with interreligious dialogue. To sit people down opposite each other and ask them to represent their religions is rather like sitting the same people opposite each other and asking them to "represent" their families. An afternoon spent in the midst of family, while you all climbed a mountain or went to the circus, would probably teach you much more about the nature of the family in question than an exchange of descriptions. Likewise, it is often extremely enlightening for religious people to speak together about a subject that is not, in full-frontal terms, "my religion."

One of us has taken part in more than his share of organized dialogues, those based in academic settings and those sponsored by church or ecumenical groups. He observes that in many respects such organized, formal events come into existence in an artificial attempt to supply the profound lack of "accidental" relationships and conversations. Fruitful and necessary as such occasions are, they rarely duplicate the benefits of unprogrammed learning—except in the peculiar but real instances where the "task" of interreligious dialogue itself becomes a kind of shared job, around the edges of which (at meals, on planes, in coffee breaks, settling logistical arrangements) the participants focus on something else. When asked to give examples of what they have learned in such dialogues, several participants will refer to those kinds of experiences for every one that quotes a paper presented or a panel discussion remembered.

These observations are not meant as objections to formal dialogue but as a clue to paths by which interfaith learning and conversation can become more common and accessible. Many people sincerely desire interfaith engagement. For them the barriers are an uncertainty about how to proceed and an apprehension about their preparation for the experience. These anxieties run the range from concern that one is not knowledgeable (or committed) enough in one's own tradition to represent it to fear that ignorance about others will lead to embarrassment or offense, from worry that another faith may be presented so attractively as to weaken ours to suspicion that others may focus only on the idealized image of their religion while we apologize for the failings of our own. Most of these barriers are only heightened the more that the dialogue in view is the direct sort.

## One Degree of Separation

Where religious differences are approached head on, obstacles can loom large. The more cultural and political tensions that exist around particular relations (and this is certainly true today of relations among Muslims, Christians, and Jews), the more dramatic this dynamic seems to be. The very features that make dialogue imperative make it daunting. In the ordinary settings where these barriers are most intimidating, nothing can help nurture dialogue more than examples of concrete strategies to overcome this dilemma. What is most important is that the steps involved are those that require no special expertise (and can be seen not to require it) and that the activity can likewise be readily seen not to involve what we have called direct dialogue but dialogue with one degree or dimension of separation. An illustration of what I mean by one degree of separation could be drawn from the experience of Jewish-Christian learning that has accompanied the partnership between our school, Andover Newton Theological School, and Hebrew College. Hebrew College purchased a portion of land on the Andover Newton campus and relocated there. From the beginning of this development, the two independent institutions engaged to build and model a cooperative relationship. The faculties met together over several years before the actual physical relocation. For many, these exchanges led to a new level of dialogue—not because we have spent much or most of our time in formal dialogue but because we have worked together on numbers of common issues and practical concerns. Our differences and commonalities in faith have been illuminated tellingly and unexpectedly when our attention was on something else.

To take a specific example, the two schools jointly sponsored a conference whose focus was on educating religious leaders who could address the need for community formation around distinct religious identity and also lead and equip their communities to participate constructively in a pluralistic society. That is, the conference addressed a common challenge that both our schools and traditions face. Its primary topic was not Jewish-Christian relations, but by virtue of talking about this common challenge together, it became a profound opportunity for mutual learning and dialogue. Another example comes from the Interreligious Center on Public Life, an institute formed as a common project of Hebrew College and Andover Newton Theological School. The center sponsors an international summer school on religion and public life.[2] The summer school organized a project that brought together Muslim, Christian, and Jewish young people to work together on the physical reconstruction of places of worship destroyed in the Balkan conflicts. During days dominated by the shared labor and the countless practical problems that this work involved, the participants found that religious dialogue was an equally constant feature, permanently resident in everyone's peripheral vision, we might say. In these cases, it is not at all a matter of changing the subject from interfaith discussion. It is the less linear path that leads into the heart of the subject.

If these observations offer at least one helpful perspective on approaches to dialogue, how might they be applied practically at a grassroots level? In the balance of this essay, we would like to highlight one model that incorporates many of the elements we have noted but that can be readily implemented in many different settings. The model is that of a book discussion group. In recent years there has been an explosion of such groups, of many types. For our purposes, the key aspect of this model is that it does not approach interfaith dialogue directly. It brings together people of various faiths to talk about books, but the books (by specific choice) are not necessarily focused directly on "religion." They depict the lives, literature, and history of people who live in faith. The group is made up of people belonging to the three Abrahamic traditions, discussing books whose characters and settings are entwined with one or more of these traditions. Religious pluralism is built into the process. Its reality is inescapable, but it is not the explicit and immediate focus. That focus is a book that stands at one remove from the actual participants. The topic is the characters and the story and the world presented in the text, to which each reader has his or her own response. In sharing those responses, dialogue is the implicit curriculum but never an imperative imposition.

**Getting Started**

The inspiration for the particular group in question was an interfaith service for Jews, Muslims, and Christians held on the night of September 11, 2001, at First Church (United Church of Christ) in Cambridge, Massachusetts. One of us attended that service, and the shock of the attacks that day and the awareness of the religious divisions surrounding them sparked an idea in her. The idea was to gather women of the three Abrahamic faiths for a monthly book group with the goal of learning about each other's faith traditions. In what follows, she tells the story of how the group (which adopted the name "The Daughters of Abraham") learned to function and some of the wisdom that might help others find their own way in such a project.

Although one person (a Christian) had the idea for the group, it became clear that the group would cohere only if women of all three faith traditions worked together to form the group. One of the prospective members (who had had extensive experience in interfaith dialogue) early on suggested the need for all three faiths to be represented in the leadership at every stage, and this proved to be invaluable advice.

We tried to have a balance of Jews, Christians, and Muslims in the group, although we found achieving this goal to be an on-going process. There was much to learn. For example, at first, the Jews and Christians in the group were not aware that for some Muslim women, particularly those from Middle Eastern countries, traveling alone to attend a night meeting could be problematic. We learned to offer rides where necessary.

It took several meetings to get organized. We had to agree on the ground rules. It became clear that no one wanted this group to be a forum for political discussion. Members wanted to stick to religious themes and seemed genuinely interested in learning more about each other. We wanted everyone to feel safe in the group. One strategy to foster a sense of safety was to adopt rules for our discussions, a kind of discipline for our conversations, based on advice given in a book about book groups, *The Reading Group Handbook*.[3] At first, we asked each member to read a chapter from this book, "The Art of Discussion," which recommends following certain rules of engagement during the discussion. Later we all read Kay Lindahl's "Listening in Dialogue," which distinguishes between discussion and dialogue.[4] Eventually, after three years of meetings we arrived at the following rules: Listen to each other (it's harder than you think); no interrupting, monopolizing, criticizing, or attacking another member or a faith tradition (particularly including a denomination or group within your own tradition, such as an anti-Catholic remark by a Protestant); speak from personal experience, rather than making broad statements; speak up if someone hits a sore point; and, finally, assume that we are not enemies.

We decided not to pray together. One of the members was vehemently opposed to this attempt and so we dropped the idea.

One person volunteered to lead the discussion and serve as timekeeper. The group leader was responsible for the flow of the discussion, keeping the group on track, asking questions to move the discussion along. If any members had not spoken by the end of the discussion, the leader would encourage them to contribute if they so wished.

We set a regular meeting time, the third Wednesday of every month from seven to nine in the evening. We tried to adhere to the agreed-upon timeframe. For some, having clear times for beginning and ending each meeting was very important (particularly for those with young children and for our hosts). We agreed that we would meet at seven, socialize for thirty minutes, discuss the book for an hour and then, depending on the evening, spend the last thirty minutes talking about choosing the next book, alerting others to special events that might be of interest, dealing with problems or new suggestions, and, on occasion, continuing to discuss the book.

Books were selected by majority vote, although if any member strongly objected, we did not choose that book. Members were encouraged to look for books that the group might enjoy reading. Over time we developed a large list and have now created a sub-list of those books on the list that we consider "high priority."[5] We agreed that we would alternate reading books that in some way related to Judaism, Christianity, and Islam.

Food became an important part of our gatherings. In fact, one of our members co-authored a book, *The Book Club Cook Book* (in which our group is featured), that notes the importance of food at book groups around the country.[6] We took turns bringing food and sharing our special recipes. We learned only to bring snacks that conformed to *kosher* and *halal* standards so that everyone could enjoy them. We ate at the beginning of each meeting, during the informal gathering time. Members arrived at various times throughout the half-hour period. Each person was greeted and offered a nametag and some food. Personal announcements were made during this time: "I'm adopting a baby!" "My dissertation was accepted!" "I quit my job!" We grew closer as we ate together and learned about each other's lives.

**What Happened**

The group developed in surprising ways. We learned to appreciate all the creativity members brought to the group and to trust what emerged.

As noted, one member decided to write a book about book groups. Two other members had the idea of traveling together as an interfaith group. As a result, a trip was organized to Andalusia, Spain, in 2005, and another, to Jerusalem, in 2006. There were many invitations to attend concerts, movies, and art exhibits that related to our discussions and invitations to more personal events, such as bar mitzvahs, weddings, and naming ceremonies. There were invitations to visit each other's houses of worship and to join Muslims in feasting at the end of Ramadan.

As we came to know each other, we shared our joys and sorrows, learning how each tradition provided support for such life events. The death of the mother of one of our Jewish members prompted a long discussion about our different approaches to death and grieving. Illness and trauma brought us together. One Jewish member shared her top ten psalms to comfort a Christian member who became ill.

An unexpected development was the use of e-mail to communicate outside of meetings. Members voted to join a computer listserve so that we could easily communicate between meetings. All of our e-mails to group members were saved on the listserve. We also posted information on this site, such as our book list and member list. One of the members took responsibility for sending out reminders of the next meeting time and the books we were reading. Several e-mail "threads" raised interesting issues.[7] In one of these threads, a Jewish member objected to the choice of a book that has an unflattering portrayal of Orthodox Jews. She reminded the group that, although she is not now Orthodox, her mother was. She therefore found it painful to read a book with Orthodox Jews portrayed as "them." A Christian member empathized, and a Muslim member concluded the thread, commenting that she could find very few books about the "normal" Muslims she knew. In another e-mail conversation, a Christian member sent her condolences to a Jewish member on a death in the family, but then confessed "I don't know what is appropriate to say." The Jewish member wrote back: "Avoid references to heaven and don't send flowers!" It became clear that exercising restraint was just as important when writing e-mails as when we spoke directly to each other in the meetings. The tone of our e-mails was key. We learned to be careful and respectful and to avoid "ranting."

**The Discussions**

The group leader often started the discussion with a general question, such as "What stood out for you?" or "What surprised you?" The leader was also prepared with more specific questions, if needed, although generally the discussion took on a life of its own. Members were encouraged to read from the book, drawing attention to specific passages to support their points.

It is difficult to represent the nature of such wide-ranging conversations, but we offer at least a few samples. Reacting to Annie Lamott's autobiographical *Traveling Mercies*, a Jewish member noted, "I learned about the importance of Jesus for Christians. It seems to be a religion for sinners; you don't have to be good. The author is saved but mixed up. I see the importance of grace and forgiveness for Christians." When the group read the novel *Lying Awake* (the story of a Catholic nun who sees visions), a member asked: "Is this spirituality or madness?" Another member commented that this book raises the question of how devout, observant people of any faith can live in the everyday world. She asked, "What if you want to say 'Peace be with you' but the world is saying 'Have a great day'?" The discussion turned into a reflection on what it means to be a person who seeks to devote a life to faith, in the midst of a society that may view that devotion in negative terms.

Our group read Maria Rosa Menocal's *The Ornament of the World: How Muslims, Jews, and Christians Created a Culture of Tolerance in Medieval Spain*. Many of us were surprised to learn of the "*Convivencia*," the time when Jews, Christians, and Muslims lived together in relative harmony in Andalusia, Spain. Someone noted that the suppleness of the culture and society at that time is hard for us to imagine today. A Jewish member noted that she learned that "We have a shared history" and "The Muslims were once *avant garde!*"

On another occasion the text was *Daughters of Abraham: Feminist Thought in Judaism, Christianity, and Islam,* edited by Yvonne Yazbeck Haddad and John L. Esposito. One member particularly liked this book because it was about all three of the "daughters." Our shared roots were emphasized. On reading the interpretation of the story of Hagar in the book, a Jewish member noted, "Reading about Hagar made me feel bad for the Palestinians for the first time. It all started so long ago with Hagar and Ishmael's exile." At one member's suggestion we read the story of Hagar, first from a Muslim source and then from Genesis.

When we read Bruce Feiler's *Abraham: A Journey to the Heart of Three Faiths*, the book prompted a general discussion about how we value our discussions. A Christian member who was a doctoral student stated, "I study comparative religion, but this is where I live it." Another member said, "I have no other group of women interested in faith to talk to. Faith is not 'p.c.' [politically correct]." Two Jewish members commented: "We are learning that there are different kinds of Christians. We thought you were just all the other (the group we have had so much Antisemitism from, a monolithic group that all basically think alike), but now we see that you have all these different groups."

## Some Reflections

Since the beginnings of the Daughters of Abraham, three other groups have been formed, and others may follow. Much of this experience is special to the individuals involved and its particular context. Every group will not end up organizing trips to Spain or Jerusalem! One of the things that catches the imagination of those who learn about this experience is the simplicity and accessibility of the process. No experts are needed, nor any guest presentations. The preparation does not require much beyond what an interested reader might be doing in any case. The participants do not need to represent any experiences but their own. The immediate subject for discussion is a fictional character or a historical period or the shared experiences of women. This allows for religious diversity to be explored as part of the whole texture of life.

As this brief description of the Daughters of Abraham makes clear, it is very important that it is a group of women. The path to religious dialogue is opened by a shared curiosity about the experience of women in various settings and also by a focus on hospitality and mutual care. The spread of book groups in general has in large measure been fueled by women who find the format particularly well suited to build relationships as well as to provide education and stimulation. The dynamics will vary for mixed-gender groups or for male groups. Nevertheless, this is one of the best models that we know to offer to those who want to make interfaith dialogue a reality at the concrete level, dialogue that will leave its mark not only in the ignorance dispelled but also in the relations established.

## Notes

1. With thanks to Rona Fischman, Anne Minton, Mary Luti, and other members of the "Daughters of Abraham" who contributed to this article.

2. For more information, see http://www.interreligiouscenter.org/educational_programs/summer_school.html.

3. Rachel W. Jacobsohn, *The Reading Group Handbook* (New York: Hyperion, 1998).

4. The essay can be found at http://www.uri.org/option,com_docman/task,doc_view/gid,16.html.

5. The appendix to this essay lists the books that the group has read to date.

6. Judy Gelman and Vicki Levy Krupp, *The Book Club Cook Book* (New York: Jeremy P. Tarcher/Penguin, 2004).

7. The listserve is a secure environment, so that members are assured of the "privacy of their conversations."

## Questions for Reflection

1.   The authors propose that indirect approaches to interreligious engagement often work better than a direct approach. What do they mean? What misapprehensions can accompany a direct approach? Have you found the authors' concerns to be valid? What experiences of an indirect approach to interreligious engagement have you had?

2.   Name some books and films that could foster an indirect approach to dialogue.

3.   Is there a benefit to "women only" and "men only" settings for dialogue?

4.   Based on this chapter, what characteristics of active listening need to be applied to interreligious-dialogue exchanges?

5.   How might food be incorporated into interreligious-dialogue activities?

6.   Tell about some of the threads that you have observed developing during interreligious-dialogue experiences.

7.   If you felt safe and at ease, what personal observations might you make to members of another tradition about their religion? What observations can you imagine people of another tradition making about yours?

## Suggestions for Action

A.   Identify projects that young people from various faith traditions might engage in that would foster dialogue, mutual respect, and trust.

B.   Put together a program with members from other faith communities that would meet the goals of "indirect dialogue" as described in this chapter.

C.   Begin a book-discussion program that would also provide opportunities for interfaith dialogue.

## Books Read by the Daughters of Abraham

*Fiction*

Godwin, Gail. *Father Melancholy's Daughter.*
Read in February 2004.
The daughter of an Episcopal clergyman comes to terms with her mother's desertion.

Godwin, Gail. *Evensong.*
Read in February 2004.
The heroine of *Father Melancholy's Daughter* faces challenges concerning her marriage and her ministry.

Kellerman, Faye. *The Ritual Bath.*
Read in January 2003.
In this detective-fiction novel, an Orthodox Jewish woman and a Baptist policeman share an interest in love and mystery.

Rosen, Jonathan. *Joy Comes in the Morning.*
Read in March 2005.
A female rabbi falls in love with a secular Jewish man. This contemporary American tale addresses topics such as issues of faith, ethics, creating a Jewish home, observance of rituals, and the balance of public, rabbinic, and family life.

Salzman, Mark. *Lying Awake.*
Read in May 2003.
A woman mystic faces serious illness and difficult decisions.

Steinberg, Milton. *As a Driven Leaf.*
Read in April 2003.
This historical fiction, set in the first century, follows the life of a young rabbi who participated in the writing of the Talmud.

Stollman, Aryeh Lev. *The Far Euphrates.*
Read in October 2005.
This novel uses biblical and kabalistic language and imagery to touch on issues of life and death, intellect, and faith through the story of a Jewish boy in Canada, post-Holocaust.

*Nonfiction: Autobiography, Memoir, and Essay*

Ahmed, Leila. *A Border Passage: From Cairo to America—A Woman's Journey.*
Read in December 2002.
In this memoir, an upper-class Egyptian woman speaks about growing up

in an Egyptian/Turkish family in the 1950s, going to college in England, and understanding the complex identity of Egyptian women in her time.

Buber, Martin. *Tales of the Hasidim.*
Read in September 2004.
This collection contains stories on the lives of the Hasidic masters.

Feiler, Bruce. *Abraham: A Journey to the Heart of Three Faiths.*
Read in January 2004.
This work explores Abraham, the father of Islam, Judaism, and Christianity.

Gallagher, Nora. *Things Seen and Unseen: A Year Lived in Faith.*
Read in April 2005.
This work details the life of a congregation through a liturgical year.

Haddad, Yvonne Yazback, and Esposito, John, eds. *Daughters of Abraham: Feminist Thought in Judaism, Christianity, and Islam.*
Read in December 2003.
These essays explore the traditions of three religions during the past century from a feminist perspective.

Halevi, Yossi Klein. *At the Entrance to the Garden of Eden: A Jew's Search for Hope with Christians and Muslims in the Holy Land.*
Read in March 2004.
The author embarks on a spiritual quest, praying and meditating with both Christians and Muslims to better appreciate the religious dimensions of the conflicts in the Middle East.

Lamott, Anne. *Traveling Mercies: Some Thoughts on Faith.*
Read in February 2003.
The author documents her reluctant journey into faith.

Lang, Jeffrey. *Even Angels Ask: A Journey to Islam in America.*
Read in April 2004.
Author shares the American convert's experience of discovering Islam.

Lewis, C. S. *The Screwtape Letters.*
Read in May 2004.
A senior-level demon coaches his nephew in tempting people away from God.

Myerhoff, Barbara. *Number Our Days: Culture and Community among Elderly Jews in an American Ghetto.*
Read in October 2002.
This study of aging through the portrait of elderly Jews details their lives, rituals, thoughts, and wisdom.

Nafisi, Azar. *Reading Lolita in Tehran: A Memoir in Books.*
Read in November 2003.
A western professor of literature discusses her experiences with a clandestine women's study group during the Islamic revolution in Iran.

Norris, Kathleen. *The Cloister Walk.*
Read in November 2002.
After twice living with a society of celibate Benedictine monks, Kathleen Norris, a married Protestant Christian, relates her experiences, including discussions of celibacy, women's history, scheduled prayer, and festivals.

Salamon, Julie. *Rambam's Ladder: A Meditation on Generosity and Why It Is Necessary to Give.*
Read in June 2005.
This study of modern-day giving as it fits with Maimonides' "Ladder of Charity" includes examples and discussion based on people of all faiths in New York after 9/11.

## Poetry/Art/Theater

Franzen, Cola. *Poems of Arab Andalusia.*
Read in May 2005.
This collection of poems is based on the codex of Ibn Sa'id, from tenth- to thirteenth-century civilization in Andalusia.

Mohiuddin, Majid. *An Audience of One.*
Read in May 2005.
This book is a collection of Islamic Ghazals on prayer and faith.

Nye, Naomi Shihab. *19 Varieties of Gazelle: Poems of the Middle East.*
Read in May 2005.
Poems about the Middle East and being an Arab woman living in America.

## Religion/Women

Ahmed, Leila. *Women and Gender in Islam: Historical Roots of a Modern Debate.*
This survey examines the historical roots and contemporary condition of Islamic discourse on gender.

Barlas, Asma. *"Believing Women" in Islam: Unreading Patriarchal Interpretations of the Qur'an.*
Read in March 2003.
The author argues against misogynist interpretations of Islam and examines egalitarian aspects of the Qur'ān.

Diamant, Anita. *The Red Tent.*
Read in June 2003.
This fictional account of the daily life of a biblical sorority of mothers and wives is told through the eyes of Dinah, Jacob's only daughter.

Smith, Huston. *The World's Religions: Our Great Wisdom Traditions.*
Read in September 2002.
The author captures the ideals of seven major faiths.

## World Religious History

Maalouf, Amin. *The Crusades through Arab Eyes.*
Read in June 2004.
Through contemporary Arab chronicles of the Crusades, the author offers insights into the historical forces that shape Arab and Islamic consciousness.

Makiya, Kanan. *The Rock: A Tale of Seventh-Century Jerusalem.*
Read in September 2003.
This novel touches on the interplay of religions in seventh-century Jerusalem.

Menocal, Maria Rosa. *The Ornament of the World: How Muslims, Jews, and Christians Created a Culture of Tolerance in Medieval Spain.*
Read in October 2003.
This historical fiction covers the rise and fall of Islamic Spain through the stories of Muslims, Christians, and Jews who lived in the region.

## Middle East History

Adelson, Roger. *London and the Invention of the Middle East: Money, Power, and War, 1902–1922.*
Read in October 2004.
Adelson examines how the modern Middle East was molded by British power and influence in the early twentieth century.

Beit-Hallahmi, Benjamin. *Original Sins: Reflections in the History of Zionism and Israel.*
Read in October 2004.
This exploration of the State of Israel demystifies the Zionist movement.

Fernea, Elizabeth Warnock. *Guests of the Sheik: An Ethnography of an Iraqi Village.*
Read in October 2004.
Fernea recalls her two-year immersion into the local culture in an Iraqi village.

Lerner, Michael. *Healing Israel/Palestine: A Path to Peace and Reconciliation.* Read in November 2004.
Rabbi Michael Lerner critiques the Israeli/Palestinian conflict and provides answers to help progressive Jews better understand and cope with the conflict.

Lewis, Bernard. *Cultures in Conflict: Christians, Muslims, and Jews in the Age of Discovery.* Read in October 2004.
Three essays analyze the clash of religions and cultures around 1492.

Pearlman, Wendy. *Occupied Voices: Stories of Everyday Life from the Second Intifada.* Read in October 2004.
This collection of interviews highlights everyday struggles of Palestinians.

Tuchman, Barbara. *Bible and Sword: England and Palestine from the Bronze Age to Balfour.* Read in October 2004.
Pulitzer Prize-winner Tuchman looks at the history of Britain and Palestine and at Britain's role in the formation of the modern Jewish state.

# 5

# Bringing the Dialogue Home

Michael S. Kogan

In this essay, I outline some of my experiences over the past several decades of trying to bring the Jewish-Christian dialogue into the lives of believers of both faiths. Since Vatican II, the new meeting of Jews and Christians has been slowly creeping down to the grass roots of mosques, synagogues, and churches. In my teaching, preaching, and involvement in interfaith projects I have tried to encourage this process.

I cover some of these activities below, without discussing my regular professional work of teaching religion courses at my university. I want to focus on what can take place out in the community to enhance the understanding between Christians and Jews. While I am a professor of Religious Studies and a writer in this field, I am also a citizen of my town, a member of a number of synagogues, and a seeker of better interreligious relations in the daily lives of people of every faith, race, and calling. I offer the activities of which I write as examples of what any of us can do to further the vital work of religious reconciliation.

## Teaching Christian Scripture in Synagogue Classes: A Unique Experiment

In 1982, Christmas Eve fell on a Friday evening, the start of the Jewish Sabbath. I had been teaching adult-education classes at Congregation Shomrei Emunah of Montclair, New Jersey, since the mid-1970s and had been devoting much thought to the theological relationships between Judaism and Christianity for much longer than that. After finishing the studies for my doctorate at the Department of Religious Studies at Syracuse University, I had joined the faculty of the Department of Philosophy and Religion at Montclair State College (now Montclair State University) in the autumn of 1973. Shortly thereafter I began to teach adult-education classes at the congregation.

61

As might be expected, the classes focused on Jewish Scriptures and history. As Director of Adult Education, I had no higher academic authorities to answer to. Thus I was free to design the courses exactly as I wished, taking as much or as little time as I needed to cover the topics I chose. A course originally scheduled to last one semester on a selected book of the Bible could be extended over several semesters if we needed the extra time to cover the material to my satisfaction. It was a professor's dream come true. Subjects, scheduling, and course requirements were all up to me. I was very happy with the situation.

And so, apparently, were the students. Some twenty to twenty-five students signed up and attended every Sunday morning for ten-week semesters in fall and spring. They were eager to gain knowledge of the Jewish faith, its beliefs and practices, its texts and observances. I began with a comprehensive overview titled "The History of the Jews from Mesopotamia to Montclair." Originally conceived as a two-semester course, it went on for six semesters (three years) and was followed by Bible and theology offerings.

Then came that Sabbath eve/Christmas Eve of 1982. Struck by the coincidence of the holidays, I approached my rabbi and proposed that I deliver a sermon that evening titled "Jesus the Jew: A Reappraisal." I believe the fact that I was, at the time, the congregation's President as well as its Director of Adult Education made it difficult for the rabbi to refuse— although, as I recall, he was far from enthusiastic.

The evening arrived; I delivered the sermon at the Friday evening service. The congregants responded with great interest. Attendance was high and the people stayed long into the night for a question-and-answer session and discussion. They had never heard of such a thing at a synagogue, and they were eager to ask all the questions they had stored up on Jesus in his Jewish setting as well as in his Christian context: Jesus as a first-century rabbi, perhaps a Pharisee of the liberal wing of the movement; Jesus as a prophetic spokesperson for the God of Israel, seeking to call Jews back from an emphasis on ritual and human-made custom to the spiritual and ethical essence of the faith; Jesus as a popular preacher/ healer/teacher among the people who threatened the entrenched power of the Temple's Sadducee elite and the Roman occupiers.

I proposed re-appropriating Jesus as a proto-Conservative Jew who (like the current Conservative branch of Judaism) recognized the authority of Jewish law while distinguishing between biblical essentials and later human accretions. His willingness to bend the tradition without breaking it and his stress on human need rather than abstract legal absolutes made his approach familiar and attractive to modern liberal Jews. I concluded by stating: "Just because others viewed Jesus as more than human is no reason for us to view him as less than Jewish." The congregation responded with enthusiasm and with an eagerness to hear more.

Having succeeded with this attempt to bring the Jewish-Christian dialogue to the grassroots level, I began to think of ways to carry this effort forward. It occurred to me that, since we had our adult-education classes already in place with a well-attended weekly program, this would be the ideal vehicle for continuing education in interfaith dialogue. We began what I believe to be a unique experiment in synagogue-based adult Jewish education—a program that offered, together with traditional Jewish offerings, courses in Christian Scripture and theology as well as in the history of the relationship between Jewish and Christian communities. I started with Christian Scripture, covering three of the Gospels, the Book of Acts, and the letters of Paul. Other courses followed. Student interest remained strong. Usually fifteen to twenty students took the courses. At a few points I had to add extra courses for those who couldn't attend on Sunday mornings.

A study group made up of Jewish physicians in the community contacted me with a request that I teach a series of classes on the letters of Paul. They had tried to read them on their own but were having trouble without a guide. (This, of course, is just what a teacher loves to hear.) It proved to be a fascinating experience with highly intelligent, articulate students so well educated in their medical field and so eager to learn about an area of thought of which they knew nothing. They were deeply impressed with the genius of Paul's original formulations. I presented Paul's theology as containing Jewish elements but in an entirely new arrangement, as if the great thinker had turned Judaism on its head. While Judaism holds that righteousness leads to salvation, Paul believes the opposite. For him, first one is saved by an act of divine grace—an unmerited gift from God. Once one accepts this gift, one is "born again," having allowed God in Christ to enter one's being, displacing ego as the motivating force of one's actions. Now one can say with Paul, "It is no longer I who lives, but it is Christ who lives in me" (Galatians 2:20). This is salvation. Righteous deeds will now issue from the saved sinner who is motivated by Christ within, living his selfless life over again, as it were, in and through the newly redeemed "babe in Christ."

Of course, Paul would say that the Jews are correct that righteousness leads to salvation. Their error is in thinking that this righteousness is a human possibility. No, according to Paul, it is Christ's righteousness on the cross—the only truly selfless deed ever performed—that is salvific. We are saved by our faith, our acceptance of this divine righteousness as a gift, which God, through grace, counts as *our* righteousness. When we accept the gift, Christ enters us and purifies our motivation, making it possible for the first time for us to act righteously. Thus Christ's divine righteousness, accepted through human faith, leads to human righteousness. The doctors were amazed at this inversion of Jewish thinking. The categories are the same, but the order of things is reversed.

First of all, Judaism does not believe in a view of original sin that renders human beings incapable of righteousness. For Judaism sin is what we do; for Paul sin is what we are. We can stop doing what we do; we cannot stop being what we are. Adam sinned. The result, according to Judaism, was that we, his descendants, got into the habit of sin. This habit can be broken with the guidance of Torah. Judaism and Paul agree that an act of grace is needed, but for us the act is far less radical than it is for Paul. The gift of Torah, a divine act of grace, assumes that human beings, even after Adam's sin, are capable of righteous conduct, even righteous motivation, if guided properly by the Law of God. After all, God appeals to Cain's righteousness to lead him to emulate his brother. God points out that Cain has free choice regarding his brother. It is true that Cain fails to act righteously, but his freedom is assumed. His sin was not necessary. Also remember that Noah is called "a righteous man." He is saved.

Other verses in the Bible could be quoted to support Paul's position, however. In Romans 3:10 he quotes Psalm 14:2–3, which states that God, looking down upon humankind, sees that: "They have all gone astray, they are all alike perverse; there is no one who does good, no, not one."

For us sin is inevitable, but, for Paul, sin is necessary.

In teaching Paul to a class of Jewish laymen, my purpose was not to demonstrate Judaism's superiority but to educate them in the thought of a great theologian and to illustrate the fascinating divergences between Judaism and Pauline Christianity. They were amazed to discover that this theory of human depravity, seemingly so alien to Judaism, can find support in ancient Jewish texts. It is true that many more biblical verses speak of the possibility of human righteousness than deny it, but Paul's thought is hardly foreign to Judaism. The differences are really a matter of emphasis.

The students were also intrigued to discover another example of how Paul reverses the order of Jewish concepts. Judaism holds that good deeds, as they are performed, filter inward, as it were, purifying the motivation of the doer of the deeds. The very structure of our basic form of prayer indicates this. "Blessed are you, Lord our God, King of the universe, who makes us holy through your commandments and commands us" (to perform such and such a commandment). This prayer is recited before performing a righteous deed or fulfilling a divine command, but look at its claim. It holds that, through the deed in question, the deed we perform as we are commanded, we are made holy. The righteous act purifies the motivation; the external deed makes holy the inner life. Don't worry about your motivation for doing a good deed. Just do it! You will find that, as one becomes accustomed to acting righteously, one's motivation will be purified. ("Purify our hearts to serve you in truth.") Don't worry about why you perform the good deed, whether you do it for the sake of the good or to make yourself feel righteous. After all, it is natural that a good person will feel good if he or she does good. A bad person feels good when he or she does evil. Surely we would not expect a good person to feel *bad* because of doing good. If we wait for an absolutely pure, selfless motivation before doing good, we'll never get around to the deed but will obsess endlessly about the purity of our motives. Judaism teaches us to do the deed. In time we will, as it were, internalize its goodness, thus purifying our motivation.

Paul, on the other hand, holds that first the heart must be made pure by the inbreaking of Christ. Only then can the deeds issuing from a human being be truly good. For him, the purified motive purifies the deed. For Judaism it is the other way around. The good deed eventually purifies the motive. What else can we mean by the prayer: "Make us holy through your commandments"? Here is another instance where Judaism and Pauline Christianity seem to be the reverse of each other. There is truth in both theories. They are two takes on the relationship between motive and act. Perhaps we need both of them to grasp the great complexities of these psychological/ethical issues. The students plunged eagerly into these debates, and both they and their teacher emerged the wiser.

Meanwhile the Sunday morning students were continuing to wrestle with issues raised in the Gospels. With whom did they sympathize: with Jesus or his opponents among the Pharisees or the Sadducees? Is the Gospels' depiction of the Pharisees accurate? After all, today's rabbinic Judaism is the heir of Pharisaic thought. Was Jesus correct in relaxing the ritual laws (Sabbath observance and perhaps kosher requirements) while strengthening moral laws (preaching against divorce or lustful ogling of women)? What about his celibacy and poverty or his focus on the individual rather than on the people Israel? Is this later issue a fundamental distinction between Judaism and Christianity? Does the latter have much to teach us about individual spirituality? How many Jews will go into a synagogue to pray alone? Is this a practice we should try to develop, inspired by the many Christians who do this? How many Christians have the strong sense of religious community so common among Jews? Should

Christians try to develop a sense of being a spiritual family similar to the Jews? We concluded that Jews and Christians have much to teach each other for the mutual enrichment of both communities.

We searched in these classes for Jewish patterns of thought expressed in the Gospels as well as for Hellenistic ideas, which, in Christianity, combined with Hebraic traditions. Judaism attempted to weed out alien influences; Christianity spread across the world because it accepted and baptized such foreign ideas. This difference brought up the whole question of our responsibility to the whole human race, our relationships to the outside world. Abraham was called to be a blessing to all the families of the earth (Genesis 12:3). Judaism and Christianity have both tried to obey that divine commission, each in its own way. One is a witness people; the other is a missionary people. How do these two patterns of conduct relate to each other and to the larger project of the world—redemption—of which both peoples are a part? Stimulated by this question, the class went on to wrestle with how each faith influences the other. Can Judaism, with its continued waiting for the messiah, protect Christianity against spiritual triumphalism born of the assumption that the world is already redeemed? Does Christianity need the "not yet" aspects of Jewish thought to prevent it from sinking into a religious complacency and accommodation with the world? Likewise, students asked, does Judaism need Christianity to fend off its tendency toward spiritual self-ghettoization? The mission of Israel is world redemption. Jews seek not to make the world Jewish but to lead it to a universal morality often referred to as the "Kingdom of God." At times Judaism has forgotten this and turned inward. However, the world-embracing mission of the church can inspire us to remember that we, too, are a world-redeeming people called to proclaim the One God and God's universal reign of righteousness. In short, here, too, we need each other to become fully what we are.

All these and many more issues have been dealt with in these ongoing courses. For me the theological issues are the most interesting, but for many of the students the history shared by the two faiths has been of central concern. We have covered this often-painful subject in depth. From its beginnings, Christianity has been deeply ambivalent toward its Jewish origins, even though the validity of Christian faith rested on the validity of prior Jewish claims. The story of the life of Jesus in the Gospels is written so as to repeat and recapitulate the story of the people Israel in Jewish Scriptures. However, if the ancient Israelites are viewed with reverence in the Christian Scriptures, the Jewish contemporaries of Jesus are often viewed with contempt. While Jews are painfully aware of the anti-Jewish polemics of sections of the Christian Scriptures and of much of the Christian tradition, they are not aware of the hostility of Jewish authorities to the nascent Nazarean movement of the first century. The Sadducee leaders opposed Jesus and the early Christians, and the Pharisees joined in once the antinomian views of Paul became mainstream within the church. They viewed this new Jewish sect of Nazareans as a heretical movement within the Israelite faith, while the Jews who followed Jesus saw themselves as the new and true Israel. Mutual hostility was inevitable.

The challenge for my classes was not to decide who was most to blame but to understand what had happened and resolve to be part of a new irenic solution to this age-old problem. Hans Kung, prominent German theologian, has said that there can be no peace in the world until there is peace among the religions. My students came to realize that they could become actors in the great drama of mutual reconciliation that is the Jewish-Christian dialogue. This work is of supreme significance for the world. If Jews and Christians can reconcile, then peace among other religions that have not had two millennia of mutual hostility can do so. This reconciliation is the hope of the world.

## A Congregant Objects

I would be dishonest if I did not report that our educational experiment disturbed a few in my synagogue. One day during the penitential season known as the Days of Awe (between Rosh Ha-Shanah and Yom Kippur), I received a memorable telephone call. The Days of Awe are set aside for reconciliation. Before we approach God on Yom Kippur for forgiveness of our sins of the past year, we are commanded to apologize to anyone we have harmed over the twelve months since last Yom Kippur. This act of contrition is not easy. We are to write or telephone or meet with those of whom we must ask forgiveness. So it was that during this period, about ten years after I began the Jewish-Christian courses, the phone rang. A prominent member of the congregation was calling to apologize. I responded that I knew of nothing for which he had to ask my forgiveness. He told me that he had been enraged by what he took to be my propagandizing for Christianity in the synagogue. Viewing Christians as enemies and persecutors of the Jews, he had been denouncing me as an agent of the "Jews for Jesus" to anyone who would listen. Having spoken with many of those who had taken the courses, however, he now understood that my intentions were far different from what he thought them to be. He apologized.

This learning experience brought home a difficult truth in doing interfaith dialogue. The issue for Jews is not Christian theology and certainly not Jesus or Paul but, rather, is the history of persecution that has caused Jews to distrust Christians so deeply. Such Jewish attitudes are all too understandable; it will take a long time before suspicions fade away. That reduction of distrust is, of course, one of the goals of the dialogue.

## The Interfaith Committee of Essex

Opportunities have arisen beyond my home congregation to bring the Jewish-Christian conversation down to the grassroots level. For a number of years in the 1980s, a local group of Jews and Christians called the "Interfaith Committee of Essex" sponsored a series of public forums at synagogues and churches in Essex County, New Jersey. A local Christian clergyman and his Jewish wife had founded the committee, and the leadership passed to my colleague at the Department of Philosophy and Religion at Montclair State, Dr. Eva Fleischner, and to me. The meetings were educational opportunities for laypeople of both faiths to come together, hear a lecture or an interfaith panel, or engage in a general discussion of a wide variety of issues. From "faith versus works" to differing concepts of Jesus, from Holocaust to Zionism, from religious exclusivism to pluralism, we covered a great many issues and spent some delightful and stimulating evenings together. The only problem was that the same people kept attending, and few others seemed interested. When others did come, the discussions could easily get sidetracked by visiting fundamentalists who were opposed to the very idea of there being more than one way to truth. The project petered out after a number of years. We were either preaching to the already convinced or locking horns with the unconvincible. This is not to say that such projects should not be undertaken in other communities. For as long as they last, lectures or discussion evenings shared among a number of churches and synagogues can be quite helpful in educating the congregants in the faiths of their neighbors. Lectures followed by open question periods can be particularly enlightening. Interest may run out eventually, but the effort is still very worthwhile.

## Interfaith Thanksgiving Services

Similarly, joint worship services of churches and synagogues at Thanksgiving can be very worthwhile. Of all aspects of religious life, liturgy is the most conservative and the last to change. Today it seems to me that lectionary reform is the next step for Christian churches engaged in interfaith dialogue. Public Scripture readings that attack or denigrate the religious "other" have no place in the liturgies of those churches seeking reconciliation with Jews. The problem becomes major during Holy Week services, whereas it disappears at Thanksgiving, which is the ideal holiday for shared Jewish-Christian worship. Of course, one must be careful to avoid giving offense with hymns or readings that cannot be sung or said by all worshipers.

Some years ago a committee from a number of churches and synagogues in and around Montclair approached me. They came to see me as the Chairperson of the Montclair State University Department of Philosophy and Religion. This committee's charge was to create that year's multifaith Thanksgiving service. The service had run into trouble in the two previous years. Two years earlier it had been held in an African American church. In front of a congregation that was half African American, the guest preacher, a rabbi, began his sermon by reminding his listeners that their ancestors had journeyed to America to be free! The next Thanksgiving, at a church service where about twenty percent of the mixed congregation were Jewish, the choir began the service with a hymn titled "Just One Look at Jesus and Your Soul Will Be Healed." Clearly something had to be done. They had come to me, a teacher of both Judaism and Christianity, to see if I could create a Thanksgiving service that would say something but would offend nobody. I was delighted to have the opportunity.

I love Thanksgiving, which combines three of my great enthusiasms: God, country, and good food. For forty years I have attended the oldest interfaith Thanksgiving service in America. Started in the 1930s by three New York congregations—Central Synagogue, Christ Church Methodist, and the Park Avenue Presbyterian Church—the service was originally conceived as a protest against rising Antisemitism in Europe. With that experience behind me, I put together a service including the grand old hymns of the day (all Protestant but non-christological), added Bible readings from both Hebrew and Christian Scriptures (Jesus can certainly be quoted in this context), and included prayers offered "in the Lord's name," which, of course, could be interpreted however the individual worshiper chose. I was so eager not to divide the congregation that I did not include the President's Thanksgiving proclamation lest that offend members of the other political party. Instead, I inserted the original Thanksgiving proclamation of Governor Bradford of Plymouth Colony. Who could object to that? The preacher of the day was carefully chosen and was briefed beforehand. ("Offend no groups present. If you must offend individuals be sure to offend all of them equally.") All went smoothly at what turned out to be a successful evening of fellowship and shared worship. Such community interfaith events are splendid opportunities for celebrating our common convictions in the embracing spirit of American respect for all faiths.


## Teaching Church Classics

Over the years I have been invited to teach Scripture classes at a number of churches. From an African American Baptist Church in Newark, New Jersey, where the pious ladies would march in holding their Bibles before them like "the whole armor of God," to an elegant Episcopal Church in Charleston, South Carolina, I have had the pleasure of teaching Scripture to eager adult students. The very fact that I am a Jew teaching classes in a Christian church speaks for itself. We have much to say to each other about the common texts that both unite and divide us. Our entire dialogue rests on that text. We share the words of the Hebrew Bible/Scriptures but differ as to its interpretation. Those differences offer us all the rich possibilities for profound engagement and sharing of ideas that characterize the dialogue.

But, I believe, we Jews and Christians also share the New Testament, if in a more complex way. As a collection of books and letters written almost exclusively by Jews, the Christian Scriptures tell us much about a crucial, history-making period of Jewish and world history. The world it reveals is a world of rabbis and synagogues, of Torah interpreters and yearning for fulfillment of Jewish destiny. If one of those Torah interpreters became the central figure of a new faith founded by Jews who developed a variant reading of Jewish tradition, should not we Jews find the accounts of all this as fascinating as gentiles do? This is our history. Who better than Jews can teach this Jewish story? Of course, I bring a Jewish perspective to these classes, but I also explain the various Christian analyses of the texts to the mostly Christian students. My task is, as always, to look at the reading from every side. What, I ask, does this passage mean to us as Jews, as Christians, and as human beings? It is wondrous how a class exploring the takes of both faiths on the same text can open and illuminate the mind, leading students to value differences of interpretation rather than scorn or fear them. This is what Jews and Christians can do for each other through shared Bible study.


## Guest Sermons in Churches

On many a Sunday morning I have had the pleasure of preaching in a Christian church. One Christmas, a Baptist church that was between ministers asked me to preach the Christmas morning sermon. I explained that I was a believing, practicing Jew (kosher, Sabbath-observing, and synagogue-going), but they were not to be dissuaded. Since I had already preached a Christmas sermon in a synagogue, I saw no reason why I should not do so in a church.

I took as my text a theme of Meister Eckhart, a fourteenth-century Catholic mystic and heretic (heresies are, of course, the most exciting expressions of all religions): "The Eternal Birth." It focused on what I take to be the theme of Christmas: the birth of God in humanity, the breaking of the infinite into the finite, "the intersection of the timeless with time" (T. S. Eliot). I sought to reach beyond the particular Christian symbols of the day (the holy family, Jesus, the shepherds, the manger) and focus on what the story was trying to tell us of the relationship between the divine and the human. In doing so, we render the symbols transparent and rise to a level of truth equally available to Jews, Christians, and all seekers of the Infinite Life.

I have delivered other sermons in churches of many denominations in which I have explored themes common to Jews and Christians or have analyzed our disagreement. Although there are some prayers directed to Jesus offered in these churches in which I cannot join, I have no problem participating, where I can, in Christian worship. That is because I believe that the God of Israel sent Jesus and his interpreters for the purpose of opening the Sinai covenant to include non-Jews. While my Christian neighbors in the pews around me are thanking God for sending Christ to save them, I am thanking God for sending Jesus, my ethnic and religious brother, to save them too. Not to save *me*, but *them*. Of course God is the savior of us all, but God saves me through Torah and membership in God's Jewish people (Israel, Jewish stock), while God saves them through Jesus and the church (Israel, Christian branch). What Jesus came to teach was, I believe, already known to Jews (God is in our midst—Emmanuel—God loves us, yearns for us and delivers us, who are beloved, to share eternal life as upbuilders of God's Realm). Gentiles did not know all this. Jesus taught them. He taught us, too, but he taught us to be better children of Israel while he, as interpreted by Paul, taught them how to *become* children of Israel by adoption through a virtual birth ceremony. This is baptism, a necessity for gentiles who desire to enter the people Israel, but a redundancy for Jews who are already natural members by birth of the same people. For me the truth of Judaism does not negate the truth of Christianity. Both were revealed by the same God, but at different times to different peoples. I try to witness to the shared truth of both faiths when speaking before Jewish and Christian audiences and congregations.

From peoples' reactions, it would appear that, at long last, many are ready to hear this message.

It seems to me that inviting Jewish guest preachers to speak at churches and Christian guest preachers to address synagogue congregations is a splendid way to build mutual trust and acceptance. To be effective, the speaker would have to be familiar with both traditions but would not necessarily have to be a clergyperson or professor of religion. We should all be open to hearing heartfelt statements of faith from those of other traditions as long as they respect our beliefs and have absolutely no hidden proselytizing agendas.

### Conclusions

It is crucial that religious dialogues move beyond the elite leadership of the faiths and become better known by the laity. This new openness is too important a phenomenon to be restricted to a tiny minority. Believers must be encouraged to leave fear and parochialism behind as they open themselves and their beliefs to influence by the "other." Perhaps that other tradition possesses insights ours may have missed. Every revelation of the Infinite One must, of necessity, be partial, that is, finite. This limitation is not because God is finite but because we are. Therefore, there is always the possibility, even the likelihood, that our religious culture will be enriched by contact with "the other" and vice versa. Religion-in-action is self-transcendence. This dynamic awareness is as true for the group as it is for the individual.

Our prayer book tells us that God is "enthroned above the praises of Israel." Religiously considered, all of us are finite bearers of the Infinite Life of God. We come closer to that Infinite life when we realize that we are not alone. Others bear it with us.

### Questions for Reflection

1. Jews, Christians, and Muslims express differences in their understanding of God, the nature of the human person, sin, and moral behavior. In your view, are these differences more a matter of emphasis or of fundamentals? In interreligious dialogue, how do we balance addressing both similarities and differences among religions?

2. If you are Christian, how do you feel about emphasizing "the Jewishness of Jesus"—that is, viewing Jesus and his teachings as compatible

with and a reflection of Jewish tradition? If you are Jewish, how do you feel about this approach? Is a focus on Jesus helpful or problematic for dialogue?

3. If you are Muslim, is Jesus a bridge or a stumbling block to dialogue with Judaism and Christianity? If you are Jewish or Christian, how do you feel about Muslims' claiming Abraham and Jesus to be faithful "muslims" who submitted to God's will as Muhammad later did?

4. The author claims that Jews might learn something about individual spirituality from Christians, while Christians could learn community from Jews. Is acknowledging differences among traditions such as these helpful to dialogue? How do we balance learning from others for mutual enrichment with holding onto our own traditions?

5. What guidelines would you propose for addressing the history of hostility that has existed among the Abrahamic faiths?

6. The author lists a series of topics about which Jews and Christians may differ: the nature of the divine, God's activity in the world, ethics, spirituality, suffering, mission, witness, faith versus works. How might you design interreligious dialogue sessions to address these differences? What outcomes would you hope to achieve through these sessions? Right off, what differences might you hear about Judaism, Christianity, and Islam regarding each of these topics?

7. Have you ever attended an interfaith worship service? Describe the experience. What guidelines would you offer those who prepare and participate in such services?

8. Is common scripture study a meaningful instrument for interreligious dialogue between Jews and Christians? Can Muslims also participate in mutual study of scriptures? What are some ways that scriptures can be part of interreligious dialogue?

9. Describe a possible model for a "heartfelt statement of (your own) faith" that you could deliver to a congregation of another faith tradition.

10. The author suggests that we should view the symbols of our faith as transparencies leading to infinite truths that we all share in common. Can you think of examples of what symbols work this way for you? Is this perspective on the symbolic versus fundamental truths necessary for interreligious dialogue?

**Suggestions for Action**

A.  Devise guidelines for learning about other religions in a setting where everyone present belongs to the same religious tradition.

B.  Create a variety of programs that could be used to foster a spirit of pluralism and learning about other traditions in a single-religious-community context.

# THE ART OF HEEDING

Khaleel Mohammed

I chanced upon a new cybertalk acronym recently: WOMBAT—
Waste of Money, Brains, and Time. It seems an appropriate description
for much of what passes as interfaith dialogue among the followers of
the three major Abrahamic religions. Let us face facts: All three of these
religions are based on a common formulation that includes and transcends rational thought. All three subscribe to the belief in a God who, in
supposed inimitable wisdom, justice, and love, created everything, then
placed contumacious humans as custodians of this cosmos. In the course
of history, adherents of these three religions have constructed a concept
of "the other" to indicate—in varying degrees of distancing—that which
is mistaken, misled, and basically different, distinct from a righteous,
correct "us." Over centuries, many of the followers of these religions have
debated, disinherited, disparaged, denigrated and sought to dispossess this
perceived "other" of goodness in the eyes of the Divine One. To be sure,
there are hundreds of verses in the various scriptures that enjoin respect
and even acceptance of the "other," but these verses are easily explained
away, since it seems that God, for whatever reason, can only truly love
one set of people. Based on the history of interaction between these religions, it would seem that their adherents, while professing to be servants
or slaves of the Divine One, have instead enslaved and reduced the Creator
to being the cosmic enforcer of bigotry.

The twenty-first century started with the destruction of the World
Trade Center in NYC on 9/11, perpetrated by my co-religionists and coun-
tered with an equally idiotic transgression by those who continue to use
religious terminology and imagery to mire the United States in a war it
cannot win. The market is flooded with books by self-styled scholars who
often, with little or no training, write about the conspiracy of Islam to
conquer the world and reduce non-Muslims to vassal status. Yet, amidst
all of the talk of sending suicide bombers to the West, of nuking Mecca,
of Allah being a false deity, or at best inferior to the God who sends his/

her son to die for humanity, we see people of goodwill still participating in interfaith dialogue. We have had such dialogue for centuries—but it has not resulted in any genuine harmonious interaction. I think that many pragmatists would see the effort as a clear case of WOMBAT.

Despite the sad history, I think that there is still hope for success. I would like to present what I view as some of the elements for making such dialogue useful. Some of my colleagues have written on the subject, and, while I do rely on their work, my perspective is sometimes different. Unlike these predominantly Christian, white, male scholars, I am Muslim and a person of color, but, contrary to the stereotype, I am not of Middle Eastern descent nor from a Middle Eastern country. I am from Guyana, the only English-speaking country in South America, a place where pluralism was in practice long before the term was even coined. These factors, especially those of religion and cultural background, are significant because they do make my experience distinctive. To give clarity to my presentation, I shall address these elements under sub-topics.

## The Problem of Recognition

The participants in interfaith dialogue can be likened to the prisoners of Plato's cave. They are still in the dark, seeing shadows and images. Dialogue, you see, gives the impression that the topic of discussion is one that allows rational analysis and will allow for the change of opinion as logic might dictate. As I noted at the beginning, however, Abrahamic religion transcends rational thinking; after all, the edicts and fatwas of religions do not have to conform to the norms of human logic. How can one have a rational discussion with someone who "knows" that the Qur'ān condemns to hellfire those who reject Islam? How does one rationalize with someone who holds that the qur'ānic law is permanent and must apply to every time and clime?

We come to the "dialogue" often expecting to find solutions, if not immediately, at least after a few sessions. One of the prerequisites of dialogue is an equality of power among parties, but as I showed earlier, the Abrahamic religions have created "the other" as the misguided one. If we have rejected the "others" based on the teachings of an almighty God, then, clearly, we are right and they are wrong. There is nothing to discuss except to seek conversion to our way of thought. Our presuppositions, our prejudices, our penchant for not wanting to see things in their true form are our shackles. A study of the situation, in the light of naked truth, without guile or false courtesy, would reveal that the religious practice of "othering" has resulted in the spilling of blood and extirpation of human life. We may delude ourselves into thinking we are having a dialogue, but we ought to recognize that we are seeking conflict-resolution.

At many such interactions, we will all act like good people, shake hands, even exchange a hug or two, and discuss banalities. Muslims will seek to outdo the Christians in lauding Jesus, and Christians may utter some charitable statements about the possibility of Muhammad's being a prophet. Muslims and Jews will ooh and aah as they marvel at the similarities in their faith-based dietary and sartorial regulations. Some of the audience may be spellbound, wondering how for centuries they could have failed to see their common outlook. Then, when they go home and look at the news, some of them might perhaps regurgitate the falafel or smoked salmon that they so blissfully shared with their Abrahamic co-religionists a few hours earlier. They will see the mangled bodies of co-religionists, either blown to bits by an improvised explosive device or decapitated by an aircraft-launched missile. The old expressions and old stereotypes will re-emerge: those Zionist occupiers of our holy land; those terrorist Muslim scumbags; and those two-faced Christians, talking about God's love while preaching that the Muslim nations are Jesus' second-advent adversaries.

We humans are masters of inappropriate euphemism. Why call things the way they are and scare people into reality? Perhaps we talk of interfaith dialogue in terms of anticipation: We are hoping that one day, with more knowledge and experience, our interfaith encounters will be dialogical. Whatever the case, we are most definitely not having dialogue at this point in time. I fear, however, that if I insist on talking in terms of conflict-resolution, my peers might deem me politically heretical. When I met the late Wilfred Cantwell Smith, shortly before his death in 1997, he told me he preferred the term "interfaith discussion." Out of respect to this great mind, I will use that euphemism throughout my essay.

### Why Should We Engage in Interfaith Discussion?

We have to realize that we are in an age where the lines of divide among cultures have become broken. When I came to Canada in 1974, there was no mosque in Vancouver, British Columbia. The Muslims worshipped in a tiny building on Eighth Avenue, and quite often there were not enough people to fill the building for the Friday communal prayer. Today, not only are there several mosques in the city but also Islamic schools. I mention Vancouver because the situation is like that of almost any other big city in North America. The number of Muslims in North America is estimated at anywhere from five to ten million. Many have been born here and are for all practical purposes North American. The present world situation has put Islam under the lens of the most severe scrutiny, and Muslims therefore have to be understood. Unfortunately, Muslims have been caricatured in the worst possible ways and still do not get to speak for themselves. The questions and opinions expressed at interfaith discussions often reflect the level of ignorance that exists regarding Islam. North America is no longer a Christian continent in the meaning that all other religions are minuscule minorities. Ignorance breeds hatred, and the only way to dispel such a potential cause for disaster is for non-Muslims to learn about the religion from Muslims themselves.

Many Muslims in North America, while they may have been born here, have still not understood that the classical constructs of Islamic law were designed when Muslims were in power and that such laws were in a medieval milieu anyway. While Christianity and Judaism have adapted their outlook to deal with modernity, institutional Islam, with all its various sects, still relies on outdated constructs. It was only recently that Dr. Taha Alalwani was credited with coining the term "*fiqh al aqaliyaat*"—Fiqh for Minorities—to reflect that Muslims in western countries must develop a new approach to the extrapolation of laws to reflect their condition. Few Muslims have any deep understanding of Christianity or Judaism, often confusing one with the other, often letting images of the Crusades or the situation in the Middle East affect their interaction with the other two Abrahamic religions.

Religious rhetoric seems to have become pandemic. Jim Hagee thinks that God blesses the one who blesses Israel and curses the one who curses Israel. General Boykin thinks that my God is inferior to his. President Ahmedinejad holds that Israel ought to be destroyed. Ruth and Nadia Matar of "Women in Green" think that the Muslims and Palestinians actually have no place on earth. The problem with this nonsense is that more than just a few believe in it; indeed, Jim Hagee's influence is global, and his financial resources are more than the collective revenues of some third-world countries. Ahmedinejad has the backing of an oil-rich nation to support his quest for eventual nuclear technology. The most powerful nation of the world sees its biological and medical research derailed by a president who apparently feels that the tunnel vision of his religious advisors must dictate national policy. I feel that the war in Iraq was partly driven by the eschatological prophecies of the Book of Daniel about Babylon (in modern-day Iraq). Religion seems to force us to act stupidly and do evil things. We don't have to think of global war; now, envisage cosmic destruction—a simple nuclear device in the hands of fanatics can bring us to our end. The only thing that can stem our descent into depravity is to understand and appreciate the diversity of religions, and this is going to be achieved only through interfaith discussion.

## What Are the Main Barriers to Meaningful Discussion?

The barriers to dialogue are presuppositions, prejudices, and cultural gaps. Muslims are still, for all their progress, largely behind the Jewish and Christian groups in terms of organization and administration. Immigrants from Asia or the Middle East control many of the North American Islamic organizations, and they confuse religion, their native culture, and regional politics. To go to some mosques is like taking a walk on a film set of *Ali Baba and the Forty Thieves*. People who normally wear the finest North American wardrobe seem to feel that a visit to the mosque necessitates the wearing of distinctive cultural dress. Such a practice, in a continent where we have so many different forms of "othering," only reinforces the idea of alienation—not only among different religions, but also among Muslims themselves. I, for example, was brought up to wear western clothes. My daughters are no different. They can understand a certain amount of sartorial conservativeness to visit a mosque, but they definitely have a problem being expected to dress as if they are from Asia or the Middle East. If they have such a barrier with their coreligionists, I can only imagine how much more insurmountable the barrier must seem to non-Muslims.

From a Muslim perspective and with painful experiences, I can relate that meaningful dialogue can only occur when there is equality of power. At many conferences today, Islam is perceived as an intolerant religion—sometimes overtly so, and sometimes in a more subtle manner. Well-meaning moderators often introduce me as a "moderate" Muslim. The implication is that somehow I am different from the rest of the Muslims, that they are all immoderate fanatics, and that I, in my sweet brownness, have somehow met the level of acceptability. Dare I reject the description? Dare I, by protest, reinforce the idea that Muslims are an argumentative bunch of people just spoiling for *jihad*?

I have often been put on the spot at question-and-answer time, with questioners not asking, but telling me that Islam advocates the killing of Jews and Christians. When I respond with the obvious challenge—produce the evidence—they are often stupefied into silence, having assumed all along that Muslims accepted this false idea. Edward Said mentioned that today much of what is said about Islam and Muslims could not be mentioned about any other religion or group of people without being condemned as the basest bigotry. Yet, people with apparent impunity still proclaim the vilest canards.

Muslims often add to the problem by going into apologetic over-drive and seeking to deny some hurtful truths. The late Fazlur Rahman of the University of Chicago could, as a believing Muslim, admit in his book *Islam* that some Muslims did spread Islam by the use of war. Many Muslim interfaith discussants, however, bristle at such a thought and seek to give the impression that all of the Islamic conquests were benevolent liberations or that some Islamophobes have indulged in prevarication. Questions about 9/11 are often met with denial, conspiracy theories, or requests somehow to explain the involvement of America in Arab-Israeli politics. These answers are useful only as fuel for the flames of rancor and ill feeling.

### How Can These Barriers Be Overcome?

I think that, as Leonard Swidler has noted, a prerequisite for meaning-ful interfaith discussion is that participants ought to come without hard-and-fast assumptions as to the points of disagreement. I will add that trust and not only honesty but also the perception of honesty are of paramount importance. Such honesty can only be demonstrated by the ability to indulge in objective self-critique. My own experience affords me the best proof: I have never ceased to point out the problems that besiege Islam from within. I never fail to point out the antisemitic commentaries or the disparaging concepts of "the other" in exegeses. I am also careful to show what the actual verses of the Qur'ān say and to explain them in terms of their context, literal meaning, and, if possible, intertextual relation to the Hebrew or Christian writings. Also, for the benefit of my co-religionists, I explain that I have to criticize my own beliefs if necessary, because the Qur'ān compels me to do so as long as it is to establish truth. The fact that I have been honored by an invitation to write an essay in this collection suggests that such honesty is welcomed.

Although I think that others have discussed this matter, I still touch upon it because it cannot be overstressed. Interfaith discussion is not to convert anyone to another religion but, rather, to understand. Ismail Raji al-Faruqi wrote that interfaith encounters must result in conversion—but he defined that by stating that he meant conversion to the truth, not to any particular religion. I understood the meaning of this idea when I first came to San Diego in 2003. I was invited to partake in the Muslim-Jewish dialogue, and, for obvious reasons, the Muslim participants shared their thoughts and fears with me. One woman disapprovingly asked, "Why are we meeting these Jews? Are they going to convert?" Were it in my power, I would have immediately removed her from the Muslim delegation—but I fear that, if I had used that as a criterion for removal of participants, I would have been the only Muslim representative.

## What Are Some Concrete Steps that Can Be Taken to Overcome the Barriers?

One of the main questions that Jewish interlocutors have regarding Islam is the seemingly pervasive Antisemitism within Islam. When I addressed the Conference on Global Antisemitism in Montreal in 2004, I pointed out that most Muslims, from a very tender age, learn the first chapter of the Qur'ān. I also explained that the last two verses of this chapter are often explained in a manner that promotes Antisemitism and anti-Christian feelings. Many Muslims denied the truth of what I had said. In response, I wrote an article citing proof after proof for my statement. I still receive e-mail, thanking me for my honesty in that article.

Another step that can be taken to overcome the barrier is that of avoiding stereotypes. The news media have conditioned us to accept a Muslim as a bearded, scowling, humorless Middle Easterner, often a disguised terrorist, speaking with a specific accent and spewing hateful rhetoric. I am the very antithesis of such a caricature. I deeply identify with North American culture; I take pride in dressing in a manner that is normal for the continent, and I definitely do not spout hate. The closest I come to being a terrorist is that some might consider my sense of humor lethal. The ability to poke fun at myself is one of the easiest ways to establish rapport.

One has to deal with difficult questions and interlocutors in a gentle manner. It is true that people can be rude, arrogant, and ignorant. I do not have to react in the same manner. After all, the Qur'ān commands me as a Muslim to repay with what is better, to use wisdom and gentleness in dealing with people. The Qur'ān warns Muhammad that were he harsh and severe, the people would have run away from him. I use this example to design my own approach.

I often will take a verse from either the Hebrew Bible or the Christian Scriptures to illustrate a point of morality. This familiarity with a scripture other than mine and the willingness to apply it make my counterparts know that I do appreciate their scriptures, that I do read them. What I am advocating, from experience, is that participants must be carefully chosen. Interfaith discussion cannot be one where participants go without training as to how to conduct themselves and as to what is expected. One has to know with whom one is dealing and how to share information. Are all the participants on the same epistemic level? Are they speaking the same language? By my question, I am not referring to language in terms of identity but in terms of comprehension. At one of the San Diego interfaith encounters, a rabbi, in academic honesty disclosed that not all Jews believe in God. His language was simple and straightforward. That, however, is not what some members of the Muslim delegation understood. After our return to the mosque, one triumphantly pointed out to me why God had cursed the Jews: "These people don't even believe in God." I did not even waste the time to point out that this was not what the rabbi had said. But who had erred? Was it the rabbi, or was it my co-religionist? I think both had misunderstood. The rabbi had not understood with whom he was dealing, and that many of the Muslims were not academics. The Muslim had heard with ears of prejudice.

I mentioned earlier about my background's setting me apart from the stereotypical Muslim. So, too, we have to realize that discussants will necessarily act out their cultural and educational conditioning. I do not expect the average Israeli who has a relative blown up by a Muslim Palestinian suicide bomber to divest herself of her sadness. Nor do I expect a Palestinian Muslim to feel comfortable at seeing an Israel Defense Forces member representing Judaism.

These are not nice things to admit, but both of these examples will be shaped by their experience. People have to feel comfortable with each other and not have baggage to schlep along. As a Guyanese Muslim I come to the table with no hate toward either a Jew or a Christian. My experience is different, for I owe a great intellectual debt to my Christian and Jewish teachers. I can look upon them as humans who are to be respected. Dare I say the same for a Muslim from Palestine or from Serbia? This only underlines my contention that the discussants have to be carefully selected: It is not just a process of grabbing volunteers who have time available or those who want to defend the honor of the religion with their acerbic polemic.

Many Jews would, I think, feel uncomfortable discussing Judaism in a mosque setting. Questions about Israel would invariably surface, and the Muslim congregation might seem to be ganging up on the non-Muslim. By the same token, many Muslims might feel uncomfortable in a synagogue, where questions about suicide bombers might be posed, or in a church, where the questions of Jesus' supposed return as a Muslim might be couched in terms implying ridicule. The locus of the encounter must be where there is full neutrality and balance of power. Only then can honesty and frankness be expected.

## What Concrete Outcomes of the Discussions Can Be Expected?

Since the discussions are in fact attempts at conflict-resolution, then "doables" must be presented. One of the basics of such discussions is that the most serious problems need not be discussed in the initial encounters. I recommend that a group of representatives draw up a plan as to what will be discussed. Not every attempt will be marked by success, and this may be for several reasons: We might be selecting the wrong persons; we may be dealing with the wrong topics; the venues might not be right; or the timing might not be right. I think that when all is said and done, however, we have to be realistic; no amount of interfaith discussion will ever remove hatred and bigotry among all religious players. In 1832, Leo Pinsker said that he did not, in the foreseeable future, perceive any hope for harmony. All he asked for was a tolerable *modus vivendi*. I think his words still apply.

## What Models and Experiences of Interfaith Discussion Have I Found Helpful?

Interfaith discussion occurs on two different levels: faith-based and academic. The faith-based discussion often breaks down after a few meetings, as certain stereotypes often prove themselves correct: the inability to understand the "other," the condescending attitudes of some toward others, and sometimes the collective ignorance of the parties involved. After all, an imam who claims to know about Christianity or a priest who claims to know about Islam will often rely on a faulty epistemological base. During the course of training, the imam or priest may have learned about the other religion, forgetting that such information is from the very beginning skewed, as it is structured with polemical intent. Even when one does attempt to read books outside of one's own tradition, theological constructs might not allow one to comprehend fully and accept the constructs of others. The average Muslim, for example, cannot understand how Christians can talk of monotheism and yet of the Father, Son, and Holy Spirit as a triune godhead. Christians cannot understand why Muslims cannot accept that Jesus died for their sins.

Academics in religion often dazzle us with their findings. However, such findings place them in the role of the enlightened prisoner of Plato's cave. They might often be able to distinguish between pristine forms of their professed religion and later innovations. Their problem, however, is that they have become so detached from the faith expressions that they have removed the phenomenological aspect of religion. They no longer relate to faith. When this occurs, they no longer truly represent their religion, for they are outsiders—they have ventured outside of the cave and, upon their return, cannot adjust to the darkness and shadows to relate to the inhabitants. They have become functionally blinded by enlightenment.

I believe that participants in interfaith discussion must be truly learned in the academic sense and must also identify strongly with the faith expression. In the case of Islam, this ability to study one's religion as well as live it is very important. Whereas in Judaism and Christianity, a rabbi and priest/pastor must be ordained, in Islam there is no such prerequisite for North American imams. On several occasions, I have heard imams express "Islamic" opinions that have nothing to do with the religion. This criterion of learning cannot be divorced from being an observant faith practitioner. Someone may be an academic scholar in Islam, but, if she or he does not practice the religion, I do not see how that person can be a genuine participant. In some cases there are obvious disqualifications: A "scholar" of Islamics who is a church-going Christian has basically made a rather clear statement of choice. A scholar of Islam who no longer follows the rituals of Islam has also made a clear statement of dismissal.

The speechmaking that occurs at many conferences may be useful for that one event but is, of course, useless for the billions of people who could not be present. Two of the best events I attended were the Scholars Conference and the Shemin Trialogue. At both events, scholars identified strongly with both academe and their faith. They fulfilled the qualities discussed earlier but were willing to go outside of the box to understand each other. In both cases, there were questions or attempts by some in the audience to disrupt the flow of things, but skillful moderation thwarted such efforts. Both events have planned book presentations of what was discussed, so that proceedings get recorded and distributed. People can then read and research. This, for me, is the model that will work.

## What Is the Most Important Element of Interfaith Discussion?

At conference presentations I have often observed panelists commit the ultimate error. While a co-panelist is speaking, they will be reviewing their own prepared speeches instead of listening to the presenter. They do this because they have come prepared to deliver and seem eloquent. They are focused only on their presentation. It is true that they might be in fact multi-tasking: keeping an ear out for the speaker's words while skimming through their notes. They are only hearing, not heeding. They might miss a subtle point that the speaker is making and not address it in their own presentation. One must surely come with prepared notes, but, under optimum conditions, use them as references only. A discussant ought to read notes before the convening of the panel, so that one can fully heed the co-panelists' addresses, and then the various points raised can be addressed as part of one's own presentation. It is called the art of heeding.

### Questions for Reflection

1.  Discuss the concept "the other." Are there ways of describing "the other" that are more or less contentious? Does "difference" necessarily mean "deviance" among the Abrahamic faiths?

2.  On a scale of 1 to 10, assess the world religious situation today: Are the forces of intolerance and distrust (1) or the forces of mutual respect and pluralism (10) on the ascendancy? Explain your position.

3.  Are the Abrahamic faiths irrational by nature? If their members are open to change through rational, logical argumentation, are they violating the tenets of their faith?

4.  Is interreligious dialogue a form of conflict-resolution? Should we view it as such? Do you know of an instance when dialogue was actually more conflict-resolution? How did it go?

5.  Is there a different feel and flavor to the term "interreligious discussion" compared to "interreligious dialogue"? What sense does each term hold for you? Which do you prefer?

6.  In the midst of dialogue, how do we speak about our co-religionists who "act stupid and do evil things"? Present an example.

7.  Give examples of confusing religion, native cultures, and regional politics. How should people in dialogue address these confusions?

8.  Do you find that people come to dialogue expecting, perhaps even wanting, members of other religions to fit into cultural stereotypes?

9.  Are you comfortable with the designation "moderate Muslim" ("moderate Christian" or "moderate Jew")? How do you suggest addressing that

some members of each tradition are intolerant and mean-spirited?

10. Do you believe that in America Muslims are subject to greater bigotry than Jews and Christians are? If so, should this influence how we do inter-religious dialogue?

11. What is the best way to address statements that demonstrate a one-sided view of an issue such as *jihad*?

12. Should dialogue participants be carefully chosen? If so, how would you suggest doing this? Is training necessary, or at least helpful, when preparing for interreligious dialogue? Should there be training for all participants or just the leaders?

13. How should faith-based versus academic-based dialogue events differ? If you have had experience in this area, have you found that faith-based dialogue events break down after a few meetings due to an inability to understand the other?

14. Do you believe that academics typically become outsiders to their own faith tradition, "functionally blinded by enlightenment"?

15. The author wants us to go beyond hearing to "heeding" during dialogue. What do you think he means?

**Suggestions for Action**

A.  Identify what you perceive to be the main obstacles to dialogue among members of the Abrahamic faiths.

B.  In honest exchanges between members of different religions, inevitably misinterpretations and unintended insensitivity occur. How can participants be prepared for such occurrences? How should they be addressed?

C.  Draw up a possible "game plan" for a series of dialogue sessions. Consider: place, participants, topics, session structure, and potential problems that might arise.

# 7

# THE POWER OF HOPE
Racelle Weiman

"Hope is the pillar of the world." This African proverb was taped to my laptop by my daughter and has become my personal maxim. At a recent interview in Indonesia, a reporter asked me, "Are you a messenger of peace?" I instinctively replied, "I prefer to see myself as a messenger of hope." In a world after the *Shoah* (Holocaust) that is full of infinite reasons for despair, I have found rays of hope. One of the places hope exists is where there are pockets of authentic dialogue between peoples, cultures, and religions. My life story has brought me to a deep commitment to the practice of interreligious dialogue. Dialogue with integrity, when understanding and learning are at their best, is evidence of "hope in action." I believe it has meaning and purpose for the twenty-first century.

## Asking the Right Questions

Initially, I found myself drawn to the dialogue table in order to find answers to the questions that my high school students in Israel were raising in the late 1970s. At that time I was teaching courses in Jewish Studies in the Israeli public school system. Discussions about faith would arise during the classes on history, sacred texts, and ethics. The teenagers were justly outraged at the vicious Antisemitism and violence of the *Shoah*. The shadow of the murdered 1,500,000 Jewish children remains unfathomable and even unforgivable. These surviving Jewish youth were now threatened: The *Shoah* stole God from this generation by robbing them of their faith. They claimed that they were "*broges*" with God. "*Broges*" is a deeply descriptive word that means, "I am so angry with you, I don't want to talk to you." My students posed the recurring question not *if* God exists post-*Shoah*, but what *kind* of God exists? Who wants to engage with a God who seems so remote from human suffering? Troubled, I reflected on this recurring statement of belief, which is a philosophically compelling

87

perspective. Clearly there is an "I" (the Jewish child) and "Thou" (God); this concept is unmistakably theistic and deeply personal. The root of this anger is the deep disappointment with God and the fear that the world might not be redeemable. Though they cared deeply about the covenant between God and the Jewish People, they were full of pain and mistrust, feeling that God did not honor that covenant.

Their angry disappointment had to be taken seriously. Though my own personal faith in God was unwavering, I knew that I must search for some version of conflict-resolution between God and the Jewish youth of today. I had an obligation to seek answers to their difficult and uncomfortable questions. I was reminded of Psalm 127: "Children are God's heritage and His reward to us." With what kind of world have we rewarded them?

An unexpected and peculiar change of direction happened in my quest. The preeminent Holocaust scholar at the time, Yehuda Bauer at the Hebrew University in Jerusalem, dismissed my questions. Bauer's words still echo in my ears, "The Holocaust is an historical event. We can tell you where it happened, who was involved, what happened, when it happened, how it happened. But 'why men do evil' and 'where was God' are not historical questions—*for that you will have to go elsewhere.*" I was shocked that I was turned away, but even more distressed at his advice: Was there no place in Israel, or at least among fellow Jews, to study these questions? Bauer had directed me to go into self-imposed exile to study with Christian scholars—most notably Franklin Littell at Temple University in Philadelphia. How would a Jew find answers about restoring Jewish faith in God by studying with Christians? It seemed incongruous, even blasphemous.

As I began my graduate studies in the Department of Religion at Temple University in 1979, I soon realized that I was part of interreligious dialogue in its most vibrant state and was presented with extraordinary opportunities to learn from the finest academics in this field. They encouraged me to ask the questions that my young students asked and then considered them with an honesty that was breathtaking. Some of these questions were later addressed in *Long Night's Journey into Day* (A. Roy Eckardt and Alice Eckardt, 1983). I was privileged to study with the pioneers in the field of Christian-Jewish relations: Franklin Littell, Roy Eckardt, Paul van Buren, Gerard Sloyan, and Leonard Swidler. They introduced me to Rabbi Yitz Greenberg and other independent Jewish thinkers. These were golden years of Jewish-Christian dialogue at Temple University: Graduate students joined the faculty and traveled across Germany to hold the first Jewish-Christian dialogues among university theology departments post-World War II; participation in formation and critique of national and international church documents and declarations about Jewish-Christian understanding; analysis of the Oberammergau Passion Play to purge Anti-semitism from its scripts; evaluation and recommendations for religious and secular textbooks reflecting the spirit of Vatican II.

It turned out that Bauer was right. I saw Christian repentance, trans-formation, and change. I witnessed individual Christians take up with dili-gence the theological and moral questions of the "teaching of contempt" of Judaism. I observed them labor alongside Jewish colleagues, wrestling with the issues of faith in a post-*Shoah* world, often ignored and ostracized by their own churches. I saw God's covenant living through their coura-geous actions. I was privileged to see Jewish and Christian scholars honor and trust one another. I believe that this is what Rabbi Harold Schulweiss must have meant when he said that the Divine Presence resides, not in you *or* me, but in the space between you *and* me.

## Weaving Hope into Dialogue

In order to facilitate the Divine Presence in filling the void between and among us, we require the essential ingredient of hope. Authentic inter-religious dialogue is "hope in action." Religiously guided and grounded people, who are open to encounter people of other religious worldviews as partners in dialogue, create a movement toward a hopeful, brighter light. In Proverbs 20:27 it is written, "The human soul is the candle of God, search-ing the inner chambers of our being." Real interreligious dialogue begins deep inside of ourselves, because we know the effort is worth it. Hope is necessary for us to believe that the intense work of dialogue has value in this world. Vaclav Havel, the dissident playwright who became President of the Czech Republic, wrote, "Hope, in the deep and powerful sense of the word, is the ability to work for something because it is good, not just because it stands a chance to succeed....It is not the same as optimism; it is not the conviction that something will turn out well, but the certainty that something makes sense regardless of how it turns out."

Hope requires action. "Dialogue" is not real unless it involves intense action: a generosity of spirit, open communication, and the formation of relationships. Often this evokes courageous acts and creative responses. In Jewish mysticism there is a belief that fragments of light are scattered throughout the universe, to be gathered up. Dialogue is a way to weave these sparks of light that come from a common ground: devotion to God and God's Creation. It is critical that we are aware and mindful that we weave together relationships to establish understanding, to respond to

God and to our environment. In Hebrew the word for hope is "*tikvah*." Its root source means to "intertwine strands together" or "connecting lines." Intertwining and connecting is active work, not passive. "*Hatikvah*" (The Hope) is the song written by Naftali Herz Imber in 1878 upon his arrival at his new home in the Land of Israel. Now the national anthem of the state of Israel, it is a call to action to heal the Jewish People and the world and to reach a time of all hopes fulfilled.

Hope is the enemy of fear. The beloved Rabbi Nachman of Bratzlav used to say, "The whole world is a very narrow bridge. The most important thing is not to be afraid at all." Hope ignites the courage to overcome fear, to believe in humanity, to attempt new directions, and to motivate change. Hope is the part of faith that determines that your actions are significant, that your voice can have an impact, despite the odds. When the Nazis sent trains to deport the 48,000 Jews of Bulgaria, Bishop Cyril of the Bulgarian Orthodox Church threatened to lie on the railroad tracks. He joined the rounded-up Jews of Plovdiv and, in front of the local police, loudly quoted from the Book of Ruth, "Wherever you go, I will go." In Sofia, Bishop Stephen declared that "he would act henceforth according to his conscience as a minister of Christ." He sent a delegation with a warning to King Boris III saying, "Your deeds are watched by God." Boris called off all the deportations; the Jews of Bulgaria were saved. The bishops were recognized posthumously with the medal of "the righteous among the nations" in a moving ceremony in March, 2002, at Yad VaShem in Israel. Concurrently, in the U.S.A. we held a series of major events celebrating the rescue of the Jews of Bulgaria by honoring a delegation from Bulgaria led by the current Bishop of Sofia and Prince Boris IV, grandson of King Boris III. Research bore out that it was the positive relationship between the Bulgarian Orthodox Church and the Jewish community pre-World War II that directly influenced their proactive support. Their heroism is an inspiration and model for interreligious dialogue.

Hope overcame fear when the religious communities in Macedonia accepted the 2002 invitation of President Boris Trajkovski to a high-powered International Scholars' Trialogue. I had the opportunity to participate as a Jewish representative at the conference led by Leonard Swidler and Paul Mojzes, editors of the *Journal of Ecumenical Studies*. I personally witnessed effective interreligious dialogue applied in peacemaking and in the prevention of violence in conflict zones. With skill and experience, the leadership guided the community in "Confidence Building between the Churches and Religious Communities through Dialogue." They gathered a whole array of local religious leaders who became part of good governance in the region. In the former Yugoslavia, the domino effect followed the religious/ethnic violence in Bosnia and Kosovo and was a real threat. Macedonia needed the ground prepared for interreligious dialogue to occur in a circle of both necessity and trust. The impressive international array of scholars provided this safety net, enabling local religious leaders to take courageous moral stands and to invoke a moral high ground for the future. Reluctance turned into enthusiastic participation from a sector often left out by the political hierarchy. As recently as 2007, they have renewed this commitment to seek cooperation and dialogue, and hope reigns.

**Summoning God's Presence in the Dialogue**

Partners in interreligious dialogue would intuitively answer the following question the same way the rabbis did in the Talmud: "Why, when the world was created, did God create just one man and one woman?" The answer: "So that humankind understands that we all come from a single union, to teach us that we are all sisters and brothers, and that no one is greater than any other." This concept of a common lineage, where every human being is created in the divine image, may be the first statement about equality, dignity, and worthiness of every human being. This acknowledges that God's presence is illuminated in each individual. We find the ultimate understanding of the worth of each person in Psalm 8:3–5, "What is man that You are mindful of him, mortal man that You take note of him? You who have made him little less than the angels and adorned him with glory and majesty." This core value may be the greatest gift the Jewish People have given to the world.

Interreligious dialogue juggles several conversations simultaneously. The first conversation is with God. God is sought not only in guidance and in presence but also to access the reflection of God in the soul of the partner, our "sibling." The dialogue partner is also in constant conversation within her own tradition, both in her head and in her own community. In addition, the dialogue itself is not only with the dialogue partner who stands face-to-face, but also with that partner's own conversations with God, his tradition, and his own community. Parity is essential to even the playing field fairly. Inequities must be acknowledged, addressed, and given consideration. The quest for true interreligious dialogue is to learn, and such learning takes place with an open ear, followed by an open mind and heart.

Listening is key to dialogue, and silence is as precious and revealing as silent prayer is during communal worship. Learning from a face-to-face partner reveals the possibility to enter and understand a living religious perspective and to stand in awe of both the rich variety and convergence that comes from differing religious perspectives. The hope is that each partner will explore critically one's own perspective, tradition, and community, as well as see oneself as reflected in the eyes of one's dialogue partner. This exploration and reflection is especially important for partners who identify a shared historical and social context. Exploring the Muslim-Hindu relationship is more urgent for a Muslim in India than for a Muslim in Tunisia. For Judaism, there are unquestionably critical issues in common with Christianity and Islam, as we share deeply intertwined narratives and histories, as well as a concern for future understandings and shared fates.

Interreligious dialogue should be approached with hope and sincerity, as well as with a deep thirst for learning. In the Jewish tradition, this perspective is embodied through the asking of questions. Children are encouraged to ask questions, and answers to questions often come with an illustration or a story. Personal narrative allows us to encounter others' perspectives as they reveal their most burning issues. I gain insight into the lives and hearts of others by opening up to the cultural, literary, and social worlds of others. A "dialogue of the heart" happens when I read. Each Saturday on the Sabbath I curl up with a book, often an auto/biography, which serves as a partner in profound private dialogue. Currently, for example, I have chosen to focus on the narratives of Muslims who live in western society, such as *Acts of Faith* (Eboo Patel, 2007), *The Trouble with Islam Today* (Irshad Manji, 2006), *What's Right with Islam* (Imam Feisal Abdul Rauf, 2004), and *Infidel* (Ayaan Hirsi Ali, 2005).

## Stumbling over the Blocks

These decades later, it is an even greater responsibility to work in the field of interreligious dialogue, and I still feel privileged. It has elements of both a blessing and a curse. At its best, there is an overwhelming pride in this manifestation of human achievement, closeness to God, and a microscopic taste of the Messianic Age.

It sometimes happens that in the name of "interreligious dialogue" one can have a nauseating and debilitating experience under the guise of political correctness, which is often full of vanity, manipulation, competition, and media hype, with no trust and no desire to listen. Interreligious dialogue often mirrors the process found in diplomacy. It is not the ideal, but it can be a useful model for recognizing and cultivating trust. The necessary tools and skills for effective and successful political relationships are brilliantly presented in *Statecraft* (Dennis Ross, 2007). Trust is the desired outcome that indicates dialogue done well.

In the political arena of conflict-resolution, politicians and governments can learn much by including religious leaders and scholars. In 1994, I was chosen to join an international summer program at the Fletcher School of Law and Diplomacy at Tufts University on the topic of Ethnic Conflict Resolution. My fellow students were in the fields of political science, public policy, or economics. I was the only person in the field of religion. They regarded me with suspicion, and my participation was challenged. I looked around the table where people were assembled from the former Yugoslavia, Northern Ireland, Middle East, Turkey, Sudan, and Rwanda. I asked if there were any of these regions in which religion was *not* a factor. They conceded that religion played a major role in the conflicts, but then the subject was avoided throughout the program. More than a dozen years later, after the break-up of the Soviet Union and the events of 9/11, now programs such as these often include a focus on Islam, but rarely on the relationship among religions and between religion and society. The awareness is not yet heightened enough to be inclusive. Until very recently, academic institutions and political bodies balked at including religions in the area of peace studies. Secular organizations are predisposed to think that religions are defined by the fundamentalists among them, and they also believe that conflicting "truths" are irreconcilable. After the Oslo Accords in 1994, I recall many meetings that included religious leaders brought together in Israel from the branches of Christianity, Islam, and Judaism. There was such delight in speaking freely together about God-centered existence and scripture-focused lifestyles. The self-defined secularists were aghast.

Polarization and ignorance, along with false expectations, are the death blows of dialogue. There is also the perception and concern that the face of religion in contemporary society is equated with extremism, hate, and violence, even though the root causes of the conflicts are rarely religious in nature. Dialogue rarely advances beyond an annual visit to a neighbor's house of worship or a shared holiday or event. As Jews, we have a long list gathered from an accumulation of negative experiences: fear of prejudice; concern about missionaries; vulnerability as a minority; fear of finding differences, fear of finding similarities; ignorance on both sides; and abandonment, once the going gets tough or if we "fall out of mode." An example of abandonment is reflected in the disintegration of the National Conference of Christians and Jews, resulting in the loss of its strong and proud role in multiculturalism in America. I discovered exactly what "falling out of mode" entails, when I was asked to buy books on Judaism to send to a Muslim in Bangladesh so he could teach a class on the Abrahamic Faiths. I naively visited the bookshelves of the Barnes and Noble store affiliated with Temple University at the beginning of the 2008 school year. The shelves were loaded with titles on Christianity and Islam all across the spectrum. There was not one book on Judaism. Ironically, Jews and members of other minority religions realize and fear that, in a post-9/11 world, the understandable rush by Christians to engage Islam in dialogue will lead to neglecting or even sacrificing the hard-earned gains that once were celebrated in the Jewish-Christian relationship.

**Healing a Fractured World**

This world of ours is full of wonder and greatness. Science, medicine, and technology have made tremendous leaps and push us to seek solutions for the world's problems—both those caused by humanity and those not in our hands. The religious personality must also continue to seek imaginative and courageous approaches to address the many existential, philosophical, and moral questions in our time. Dialogue is essential for religion to be relevant and to share in global conversation, generating positive outcomes that advance and unite humanity.

The future for religion lies in authentic interreligious dialogue that is global and inclusive. Religious minds must engage in the challenging ideas about globalization such as those put forth in the international bestseller *The World is Flat* (Thomas Friedman, 2005). Interreligious dialogue is an effective methodology to respond to globalization and its impact on countries, societies, communities, and individuals. If religious leadership becomes involved and adapts this new reality of a deep global engagement, it can have an important voice in social, economic, and political issues, making their impact on humanity relevant and accessible today. Cross-cultural, global perspectives that address issues such as human rights, hunger and disease, genocide, international business, and the environment would then include religion as a legitimate component. The "flattening of the world" prods Judaism, as well as the other Abrahamic traditions, to seek dialogue with all of the world's children of God, as an act of hope and as an imperative. "There are two ways to flatten the world; one is to use imagination to bring everyone up to the same level, and the other is to use your imagination to bring everyone down to the same level."

The real warriors for interreligious dialogue do not lose sight of its goals and objectives. With awe and wonder, they continue to listen, learn, hope, and create partnerships to invite God's presence. Lives full of the love of God reflect that love of God through acts of lovingkindness to other human beings, across a page, across the room, across the Internet, across the globe. The goal is to be in partnership with God, working toward a moral and ethical world, a place of compassion and justice. God empowers us to make mistakes and get it wrong. We fall, we learn, we are lifted up. "Creation is God's unfinished symphony, and He has entrusted its completion to us" (*To Heal a Fractured World* [Rabbi Jonathan Sacks, 2005]). Does God have faith in us? This question is answered by the question: Do we have faith in ourselves? For the Jewish People, the objective is to seek "*Tikkun Olam*," mending, repairing this broken world. The Talmudic dialogues of the rabbis advocated bringing *shalem* (wholeness, perfection) and *shalom* (peace) to the places where they do not yet exist. Rabbi Tarfon reminds us, "It is not for you to complete the work (of repairing the world), but you are not free to abstain from it." And Rabbi Hillel taught, "In a place where there is an absence of humanity, there one must strive to be human."

To be fully human, to be a "*mensch*" is to be most similar to God, to be close to holiness. Interreligious dialogue with integrity leads us to holiness. In the Reform prayer book of the High Holy Day services we find this prayer, woven together from different threads of our scriptures:

> Blessed are you, O God, who teaches us to love our neighbor as ourselves...many are the ways of holiness, varied are its paths. There is holiness when nations meet to beat swords into plowshares, and when people of different backgrounds work together for the common good. There is holiness when we respect what divides us and emphasize what unites us, and when we are willing to be laughed at for what we believe in.

### Questions for Reflection

1. What does the author mean by saying that the most essential ingredient in interreligious dialogue is hope? What do you feel? What would interreligious dialogue look like without hope?

2. How might members of various religions jointly address the social, economic, and political problems facing our world today? How can interreligious dialogue be applied to peacemaking and justice building?

3. Give specific examples of how interreligious dialogue has helped you develop critical thinking toward your own experience of faith and your faith tradition.

4.   The author proposes that interreligious dialogue should be approached with awe, hope, and a thirst for learning, in spite of the fear. What are the fears that are present in the interreligious encounter? Can you describe fear and discomfort you experienced or witnessed?

5.   How did the experience of learning from Christian scholars grappling with religion's role in the Shoah become a signal to the author that interreligious dialogue is a valuable endeavor? Why was it so important to her? How can we approach historical and current events in interreligious dialogue?

6.   How can interreligious dialogue play a role in globalization? What different arenas and settings can you envision the religious dialogue playing a positive role?

7.   How can people address the perception that religions are polarizing and lead to extremism, hatred, and violence?

8.   How would you describe the ultimate goal of interreligious dialogue for yourself? Do you believe that this goal reflects the core goal of your religion as well? What about the goals of other religions?

**Suggestions for Action**

A.   Identify elements of your own religious tradition that promote respect for and openness to other traditions.

B.   Describe the ultimate goal of interreligious dialogue for yourself. Do you believe that this goal reflects the core goal of your religion as well? Of all religions?

C.   Create a dialogue program centered around the themes of hope and healing in each religion.

# CONCLUSION: MAKING DIALOGUE REAL

Maria Hornung

We, the authors in this book have broken open something of our lives with our passion for interfaith dialogue. In closing, we want to engage you the reader in the critical question: How can interreligious dialogue move from the halls of academia to the grass roots where we contend it needs to be in the twenty-first century? This question is crucial. Its answer is also somewhat illusive. We need to live into the answers one person, one community at a time. Creating a place of dialogue is creating a home for the human family, a place of trust and of greater comfort, of common ground. Coming into a space of genuine dialogue is coming home.

We invite you into the enterprise of creating a more holistic human community. We need to build and to cross bridges into ethnic and religious worlds beyond our comfort zone. We need persons who are at home with people of many faiths. We need interfaith collaborations that will create universal community of humankind, of the whole web of life.

*Queries: In this book, with whom have you identified? What insights have dawned for you? What will be your next steps to engage interreligious dialogue?*

### Key Roles in the Interfaith Endeavor

Over the last twenty years, at every level of society we find contributions to interreligious engagement. It has by no means reached a point where everybody is doing it. But this consciousness and commitment have attained the critical mass where the imperative to interreligious dialogue is easily recognized in Indonesia, the Philippines, Ghana, Germany, the United States, India, Jordan, Kenya, the Netherlands, Pakistan, Uganda, England, and many other countries. The 2006 meeting of the World Conference of Religions for Peace, "Confronting Violence and Advancing

Shared Security," saw more than 800 religious leaders from nearly 100 countries gather for this assembly. They represented ten major religious traditions throughout the globe. Their reports and recommendations can be found at: http://www.wcrp.org/about/assemblies/kyoto-2006. At this point in history, all the world can see that religions with their insights into the sacred and their enunciated paths to human goodness have the power to facilitate, impede, or prevent movements to reconciliation, justice, and peace.

What these religions now cannot ignore is the imperative to engage other religions in mutual understanding, appreciation, and collaboration. Interreligious dialogue is now an acclaimed priority of the human community. In October of 2007, the United Nations established a high-level dialogue session, asking each nation to be accountable for their present position on intercultural and interreligious inclusivity and cooperation. This step is only a beginning, but it is a significant one for this moment in human history.

In every religion we can discover significant roles that impact the whole. We invite you to consider what your role is in this growing movement. We hope you can connect with one of the key roles described here and determine what your next steps can be to foster this now necessary respect for religious diversity. Key roles include: theologians, religious leaders, educators, animators, and the grassroots faith community.

## 1. Theologians and religious leaders

*Theologians* from many religions have given their lives to the search for God, to the understanding of our experience of God, and to articulation of the fruits of these endeavors across faith traditions. Some academic scholars have taken great risks to be faithful to the journey of interreligious dialogue and to the discovery of truth, goodness, and beauty across religious boundaries. So also have individuals at the grass roots taken risks; their experiences should inform the academic endeavor. The prolific works of scholars informed by the grass roots have the power to be transformative. One of the challenges we face is in making these works accessible in languages, formats, and marketing styles to the wider public.

*Religious leaders* like the Dalai Lama and John Paul II have indeed provided significant leadership in initiating and advancing interreligious engagement. At the same time, religious leaders inspire their congregants to be faithful to their particular religious beliefs and practices. In this role, some leaders have oppressed their members who act collaboratively across religions' boundaries. Others know that those who discern new interpretations of dogmas offer building blocks to a greater common ground of good for all; these broadened understandings offer the underpinnings of a compassionate pastoral approach to modern issues facing millions in the twenty-first century.

Academic theologians and religious leaders need to let go of unconditional power that can close doors to ongoing discussion. All of us need to cultivate heightened awareness in deepening the roots of our faith. Religious leaders need to identify and to train educators and animators, those individuals not in appointed roles who have the energy and interest to help create interreligious engagement. These educators and animators, in turn, can offer educational opportunities for the grass roots.

*2. Educators and animators*

*Religious educators*, who design, implement, and encourage participation in formal and informal reflective study programs also have critical choices to make. Their challenge is to design engaging educational offerings for students at all levels. Pilot program development and identifiable resources must support these offerings. It is a call that demands a terrific commitment of time and energy. Networking is necessary; enthusiastic support from leadership and passion from the grass roots make a significant impact on the functioning of religious educators.

*Local-level animators* for interreligious engagement are our hands-on workers. Dialogue between human experience on the ground and religious leadership has led to an articulation of four modalities of religious dialogue. These are: the dialogue of life or neighborliness, the dialogue of making common cause, the dialogue of shared spiritual and aesthetic moments, and the dialogue of religious doctrine and values and their integration into the world of today. These workers, however, face a myriad of obstacles in local communities: competing priorities for time and energy, a lack of awareness or interest or both, a sense of being overwhelmed by the task at hand, and insufficient religious education offered to local members and others. They need the support of religious leaders and the collaboration of religious educators.

Educators and animators need to network across religious traditions to form ministeriums of support. These in turn can collaborate to meet the needs across boundaries: 1) the need to develop models for creative and effective interactions within their congregations; 2) the need to keep their wider congregation informed of interreligious activities within those congregations and beyond; 3) the need to foster emergent paradigms to facilitate study, love, and action; 4) the need to press academics for user-friendly tools and documents.

With more of these needs met, animators will not burn out so quickly and can work more consistently to network among social-outreach ministers, youth leaders, and adult-faith educators. As these networks grow strong, our faith communities can connect with the needs of the poor, the elderly, the youth, and the civic community at large. This is a huge arena for faith flowing into action and for cross-fertilization of ideas.

One major cross-fertilization happens when theologians and religious leaders share serious conversation with religious educators and animators. Academics and religious leaders can be presenters in the more informal educational forums; the religious educators and animators are well-positioned to tailor study groups and worship occasions to the background and availability of the widest variety of persons and groups. These key players can also work together to influence budget priorities to ensure adequate allocation of funding for interreligious engagement.

*3. Grass Roots*

*Congregants at the local level* have achieved some wonderful interactions with those of other faiths. The stories of people collaborating to change patterns of structural injustice in global and local arenas have not been fully told. The Earth Charter process, developed by the United Nations, was a stunning achievement of local involvement across many nations. It remains at present the best global consensus of Earth's concrete vision for its future and the practical strategies to make the vision real.

Remarkable interfaith prayer moments and shared liturgies are more common than ever. The wisdom of experience and some of the findings recorded by theologians mitigate the fear inherent in stepping into these spaces of shared ritual. Where faith-based exchanges at the grass roots are happening, the people involved are experiencing warmth, excitement, empowerment, and hope.

At the same time, the growing tide of interfaith experiences is offset by the impact generated by large numbers of those who know little about people of other religious traditions except stereotypes generated by the media to whom they choose to listen. Large numbers remain comfortable in childhood understandings of the faith and these remain the underpinnings of their adult responses to others in life. Many do not have motivation and inspiration to move into more responsible adult faith stances. Fundamentalism and extremism are strong in almost all faith traditions on the part of congregants as well as within the other major religious roles that I have identified.

Where is the next most critical arena of interreligious engagement? Right here at the grass roots. This is where the force for world change will result in the greatest transformation of our lives. It takes the commitment of all the players to make this happen. It takes movement beyond our comfort zone of thinking, attitudes, and behaviors. It takes priority time, along with the priorities of family, job, spirituality, and leisure, to build society across religious boundaries (and other boundaries as well).

*4. Networking and finding direction at the heart of these relationships*

At the heart of any of our roles is networking across all the lines. We each must focus on the communal impact of the good functioning and good collaboration of our roles within a wholistic view of interreligious dialogue. At the heart of this point of view is the contemplative spirit that enables us to grasp something of the new creation, to have the needed courage and patience to take each step, to sense the depth of the sisterhood and brotherhood that is slowly being born, and to rejoice in this wonderful journey into the mystery of being more fully human.

We need study and planning arenas, safe arenas where working through difficult questions and issues can find a home. We need public expressions of interfaith witness and collaboration. We need religious-leader conferences. We need annual meetings of educators and animators. We need all kinds of models that move us to find and claim common ground, a growing kinship.

The Interfaith Center of Greater Philadelphia, of which I am a part, is a new venture sponsored and headed by leaders from seven differing faith communities. We live and work as friend, as learner, as inspirer, as networker, as facilitator, as animator, as pioneer. In the words of Imam Muhammad Abdur-Razzaq Miller, president of the Board of the Interfaith Center,

> Our Interfaith Center is working hard to strengthen interreligious understanding and collaboration. We realize that such understanding and collaboration is built on a deeper grasp of the values, tenets, and practices of universal love, compassion, justice, charity, and the forbiddance of evil in one's own faith tradition. It is further built on a discovery and appreciation of these same values in other religious traditions. Interfaith work is like a journey in which one climbs a mountain. The pinnacle of this mountain is the discovery not that "you are like me" but that "I am you." When this is realized, your hunger is my hunger; your difficulties are my difficulties; your illness is my illness; your happiness is my happiness and your success is my success. Out of this discovery and, hopefully, the mutual discovery of what is divine in each of us, and the mutual discarding of what is not, together we can work together for the common good. As we strive hard in the effort, we will, by God's grace, continue to learn. We ask that God bless all who engage in this work.

*Queries:* What key roles in the interfaith endeavor do you identify in your own setting? What is your role? How do you assess the interrelationships among roles with which you network? What next steps suggest themselves to you?

## Introducing the Art of Interreligious Dialogue

In the last three years, I have more fully realized how necessary it is for interreligious dialogue to move from the halls of academia to the grass roots; interreligious activity needs to find expression in classrooms, places of worship, social and political arenas, formal and informal gatherings of concerned citizens, and global forums such as the U.N. and the World Bank. The pivotal question, of course, is: How do we do this? What resources are at hand to make this possible?

In 2007, Paulist Press released my book that was written to address this question. Against the backdrop of the current world situation, *Encountering Other Faiths* draws on the contributions of thinkers in the fields of intercultural competence, faith development, and interreligious dialogue. The book develops a model for introducing interested persons to the art of interreligious dialogue. Drawn from the book, I have also designed a seminar workbook outlining the nine focus sessions and offering accompanying resource texts for the use of the facilitators and participants at any level of interreligious-dialogue work.

Inherent in this work is an invitation to all who desire to reach out to others in compassion and trust, aware that, while we are distinct from one another, we do have common ground and that together we must find that common ground. This work outlines a nine-session series that aims to introduce interested members of faith communities to the exploration of interreligious dialogue. It is an up-to-date tool for religious leaders and educators who want to help themselves and others get started on the path of sincere and transformative interreligious dialogue by first learning what it is and why it is important. Especially significant in the development of this work has been the involvement of Mahmoud Ayoub, Ph.D., Islamic Studies, Temple University (now Hartford Seminary); Leonard Swidler, Ph.D., Interreligious Studies, Temple University; and Jane West Walsh, Ed.D., Jewish educator and consultant. Persons in the Baha'i, Catholic, Hindu, Islamic, Jewish, Protestant, and Sikh faith traditions have further critiqued it.

One of the easiest ways to acquaint you with the work is to identify the nine seminar sessions outlined in both the book and the workbook:

- Session One: Gathering in Faith: welcome, exploration of hopes and expectations, and planning for the seminar
- Session Two: Assessing our Encounters with People of Other Faiths: developing insights about interreligious encounters and becoming acquainted with the ground rules of interreligious dialogue
- Session Three: Exploring Religious Diversity within Our Locale: becoming aware of other faith traditions and the implications of this presence in relation to the various modalities of interreligious dialogue
- Session Four: Treasuring Our Faith Heritage: articulating and affirming the authenticity and relevance of aspects of one's own faith
- Session Five: Engaging in Dialogue with People of Another Faith: opening oneself to truth and goodness in different religious traditions, discovering shared commonalities and differences
- Session Six: Exploring Common Ground We Find with People of Other Faiths: affirming this common ground and the nature of the dialogue that fosters it
- Session Seven: Learning from Our Personal Experiences: sharing stories of deepening faith through interreligious engagement and naming ways to share these with the wider faith community
- Session Eight: Responding to Our Call to Interreligious Dialogue: critiquing the seminar process and supporting participants in identifying ways they can assist others in becoming acquainted with interreligious dialogue
- Session Nine: Envisioning a New World Reality: deepening kinship, confirming tenets of universal love, compassion, justice, and charity within faith traditions and their potential for collaborating across interfaith boundaries for the common good

Resource readings in the workbook include the following:

- The United States and the relevance and imperative of interreligious dialogue
- Stages of faith and interreligious dialogue
- The meaning of interreligious dialogue

- Ground rules of interreligious dialogue
- Stages in the process of interreligious dialogue
- Modalities of interreligious dialogue
- Major themes of exploration for use in interreligious dialogue
- Introduction to common ground
- Spirituality: A common ground for the American people?

The workbook also contains good supports for facilitators: 1) a section elucidating assumptions and basic principles that underpin the process, 2) a facilitator's guide that offers helpful suggestions as to how the process can be variously adapted to accommodate the unique backgrounds of and various time frames available to prospective participants, as well as 3) some helpful appendices.

In the piloting of this introduction to interreligious dialogue we feel that we are working toward our objectives of 1) meeting people where they are, providing them with a secure, accepting, and affirming environment; 2) truly exploring interreligious dialogue; and 3) facilitating the empowerment of people to become engaged in interreligious dialogue and enjoy it. Evaluations of this experience highlight its applicability within both a single-faith group as well as within mixed-faith groups. The seminar supports reflection on the meanings of one's own faith as well as those of different backgrounds. The process of engaging small groups is especially helpful in modeling how to probe more deeply into one's own beliefs as well as learning how to reflect back what has been heard from others. The structure and tone of the seminar provide a safe environment. Participants are delighted to discover a number of commonalities among various faith traditions. Seminar participants report learning skills they would be able to use in various settings in their lives. Participants emerge with a deeper commitment to continue such interreligious conversations. Indeed, participants have gone on to reproduce this seminar in whole or in parts as the occasion dictates. Jane West Walsh, one of our consultants, has said: "My experience has taught me that learning about interreligious dialogue IS interreligious dialogue. I recommend this engaging yet easy-to-facilitate program to rabbis, ministers, imams, priests, educators, and lay leaders across North America who want to guide their congregants by taking that first step, together."

## Stages in the Process of Interreligious Dialogue

In my work with Leonard Swidler, who for more than forty years has pioneered in the field of interreligious dialogue, I have come to value the basic goal he states in Chapter One for this work: to learn to grow and change behavior accordingly. In that growth and change, he articulates stages of awareness. These are not necessarily linear; we move in and out of various states of awareness as our experiences dictate. I recognized in his articulation of these an exquisite match for my own reflected experience of spiritual formation. I include these in my book, *Encountering Other Faiths*, and I offer them as a conclusion to this collection. They are the key to that transformation within, from which the transformation of society will most securely and surely come. I offer them in a reflective format that invites you the reader and us the authors into a circle of friends that has made us share the best that we know with each other and able to count on a sisterhood and brotherhood with each other.

## Stages in the Process of Interreligious Engagement

Coming to appreciate the truth, goodness, and beauty of another faith is an ongoing process. Using the experience of people engaged in dialogue, Leonard Swidler has identified seven stages of genuine dialogue. In essence these are:

*Stage One: Radical Encountering of Difference*
Early encounters with those of other religions are inherently challenging and even threatening as I face a worldview, a way of interpreting reality, and ways of responding that are clearly Other. I soon realize that this disruption to my own worldview and ways of responding won't go away, nor will it accommodate to my own. I may be tempted to withdraw from the situation.

*Stage Two: Crossing Over—Letting Go and Entering the World of the Other*
As I make the decision to engage the world of the Other, I find myself called to explore, to learn anew, and to reassess my norms about adequate and appropriate expressions of values as well as to critique my traditional attitudes. I find that I need to approach the worldview of the Other with openness and with a bracketing of my stereotypes and prejudices.

*Stage Three: Inhabiting and Experiencing the World of the Other*
The sincere experience of empathy and interest then expands into a sense of freedom that opens doors to learn many things from this other

world: what is of greatest importance, modalities of interaction, what causes suffering to those in this world. As I experiment with integrating newly discovered ways of thinking and acting, I sense an excitement and a deepening relationship with those of this world.

*Stage Four: Crossing Back with an Expanded Vision*
   The new knowledge I have gained in alternative ways of thinking and acting is now part of my repertoire as I regain a sense of comfort in my own world. I am able to think and act from both perspectives as the context may require. My sense of identity has deepened, has changed, and, no matter what choices I freely make to believe and to act, I can no longer accept that my former unilateral way of being in the world is the only way. My attitudes and concerns are irrevocably reshaped to hold the Other in view, in relationship.

*Stage Five: The Dialogic Awakening—A Radical Paradigm Shift*
   I experience a profound shift in my worldview with an expanded consciousness of concerns and needs as well as causes of dysfunction in world realities. I can no longer return to my former worldview, which did not have a place for this Other. Further, I am irrevocably shaped to the possibility of a plurality of viable worldviews, concerns, and human responses. I sense the interconnectedness of myself and many/all Others, including Earth and all her needs and potentials.

*Stage Six: The Global Awakening—The Paradigm Shift Matures*
   This stage of deep dialogue opens me to the common ground that underlies the multiple worlds with which I am surrounded. I perceive that the unique differences essential to these worlds are contained in a field of unity. I embrace an expanding world of communities of life, with greater potential for ongoing dialogue and new learning and deepened relationships.

*Stage Seven: Personal and Global Transforming of Life and Behavior*
   One of the most significant transformations that takes place on this journey is a greater and more encompassing moral consciousness and ensuing practice. The communion that I experience with all—self, others, Earth—is profound. I sense that my care for myself, instead of being in competition with concerns for the welfare of other realities, is integral to the care of the whole. I experience deeper meaning in relationships and in my whole life.

*Queries: Does this process of transformation seem familiar to you? Have you thought of relating it to your own religious experience? What value do you see in opening the possibility for this learning and change in your own life and in the lives of others?*

Our overall aim in this collection has been to inspire and to encourage making dialogue real, involving the grass roots in every arena of life. The epilogue that follows includes the stories of people whose lives have been enriched by interreligious dialogue at formal and informal levels. In reading their stories, we invite you to reflect on how you may already be engaged in interreligious dialogue and, if not, where you might be. We invite your involvement for the sake of the survival of our planet and for the fulfillment of our human potential.

We trust that our sharings will animate theologians and religious leaders, educators and local leaders, and members of grassroots faith communities. We hope something in our writings matches your situations or talents or gifts. We are open to hear your insights, to be inspired by your dreams and to be encouraged by your endeavors. Please find us at the following website: www.jesdialogue.org.

## Resources

The *Workbook for Encountering Other Faiths* is available from the Interfaith Center of Greater Philadelphia. The book may be ordered via e-mail at meh@ interfaithcenter.org.

The Dialogue Institute (Interreligious, Intercultural, International) was founded in 1978 as an outreach arm of the *Journal of Ecumenical Studies*. Enjoying its unique position on the urban campus of a secular public university, the Dialogue Institute is a global leader in teaching the theory and practice of interreligious dialogue. With an international focus, the Institute works collaboratively with other universities, non-governmental organizations, and the business and public sectors to create programs and resources fostering mutual understanding among adherents of diverse religious and cultural traditions. See www.institute. jesdialogue.org.

The *Journal of Ecumenical Studies* has been at the forefront of ecumenical and interreligious scholarship for more than forty years. Based at Temple University in Philadelphia, the *Journal* features peer-reviewed articles by leading scholars across the spectrum of religious traditions, addressing key themes in contemporary and historical interreligious and intercultural dialogue. This quarterly publication also features book reviews and extensive bibliographic listings of current articles on interreligious issues drawn from hundreds of journals from around the world, making it an excellent resource for those engaged in the work of interfaith dialogue. See www.journal.jesdialogue.org.

## Questions for Reflection

1.   We might think of extensive engagement in interreligious dialogue as "leaving home." Can it also be, as it was for the author, "coming home" to God and the sacred? If so, in what way?

2.   Whom do you consider to be among the icons of interreligious engagement? Tell their story.

3.   How can your religion contribue to the creation of a more tolerant, just, and peace-filled world?

4.   Do you find most members of your faith tradition to be more exclusivist, inclusivist, or pluralist in their views on religions? What types of programs or experiences do you think might help to broaden their perspective?

5.   Give examples of possible applications of the following: dialogue of life, dialogue of action, dialogue of religious experience, dialogue of faith and belief.

6.   Have you ever experienced a transformation similar to the seven stages the author describes? If so, tell the story. Do you believe that undergoing stages such as these would be a positive experience for all people of faith?

*Epilogue*

# Building a Shared Home for Everyone—Interreligious Dialogue at the Grass Roots in Indonesia[1]

Achmad Munjid

## Introduction

Religious plurality has been part of Indonesian social life for centuries, long before the country became a modern nation-state in 1945. Islam, Christianity, Hinduism, and Buddhism are the primary traditions, but indigenous beliefs and other older earth-based religions still have passionate adherents in some communities. The influence of religion on all aspects of life, including public policy, is substantial. Yet, despite the abundance of varieties of religious expression, interreligious dialogue is a relatively new phenomenon. In this century up until the 1970s interfaith dialogue primarily functioned to provide a forum for the negotiation of "rules for proselytizing," particularly between Muslims and Christians. For almost three decades now, the culture at large views those religious leaders or lay people in each tradition who embark upon any conscious movement to promote religious pluralism as either innovative or harmfully radical. In 2005, for instance, the Indonesian Council of Ulama (MUI) issued an edict stating that religious pluralism is prohibited (*haram*) in Islam.[2] The oldest organization focusing on interfaith issues in the country is Interfidei, The Institute for Interfaith Dialogue in Indonesia, founded by Th. Sumartana and his colleagues in 1991.[3] So far, Interfidei's main projects include conferences, workshops, publications, seminars, research, exchange programs, short courses, community-service learning, and visits to religious centers. Each program is designed to promote the values of religious pluralism and the necessity of interfaith dialogue.

The following story about the work of promoting interfaith dialogue at the grassroots level is personal, for, along with my wife, I have worked for Interfidei for many years.

## Fundamental Reasons for Dialogue

In modern Indonesia there are several fundamental reasons why inter-faith dialogue is of urgent importance, especially at the grass roots. Indonesia is a land in crisis. Tsunami, earthquake, flood, drought, inflation, economic and political upheavals, extremes of wealth and poverty, unemployment, poor education, diseases, violence, and unrest have made life hard.[4] Add to this mix the reality of religious plurality. Besides the Muslim majority (some 86% out of 230,000,000), almost every other world religion has a significant number of followers in the country.[5] Depending on one's perspective, the plurality of religions contributes to the problem or to the solution. At Interfidei we promote the values of religious pluralism, both sociologically and theologically, by creating opportunities for interfaith dialogue. We want to use the rich variety of forms of religious expression as a vital part of the solution.

Indonesian people are generally religious, and religion plays a significant role in Indonesian social life. Why? Th. Sumartana pointed out that in Indonesia religion is the oldest institution of society and functions as the primary "language" known by the culture.[6] During the present time of, on the one hand, an upsurge of religious passion, loyalty, and adherence and, on the other hand, religious conflict and competition, religion clearly occupies a strategic position in the future of Indonesian social transformation. Religion can transform social life for the better only when it begins to transform itself. To move beyond the limited view of religion as a set of doctrines and to see religion as a way to link our lives to the essential energy of life take a great leap of consciousness. Through interfaith dialogue, members of a religious community can learn how to speak and listen to each other in order to have productive social interaction within a pluralistic society. The primary purpose of dialogue, argues Leonard Swidler, is to learn, that is, to change and to grow—in other words, to transform.[7] This transformation, in my opinion, is multidimensional: internal and external, theological and sociological, personal and collective. Especially within the Indonesian context, interfaith dialogue can promote social cohesion and mitigate against those forces that lead to social disintegration. We hope and believe that the kind of interfaith dialogue we are creating in Indonesia will foster peace, justice, equality, anti-discrimination, human rights, tolerance, and other principles of democracy. In short, interfaith dialogue can be a very, perhaps even the most, important contribution of the religious community toward the true civil society.

This goal is most important in an era when religious diversity can be catastrophic. When people are manipulated and thrust into situations of ideological and economic conflict that play into the hands of fundamentalists and agendas of violence, we are not reaching our fullest human potential.[8] Indonesia is hardly the only part of the world in which religious belief has fueled social calamity. Interfaith dialogue becomes an even more critical tool in this kind of potentially dangerous situation and must be properly understood and practiced by people of each religious tradition at the grass roots. The "enemy" of religious people should not be understood as the "other" or "infidel" in its old sense. The "enemy" of religious people is in fact the dehumanizing reality of poverty, backwardness, oppression, ignorance, and other destructive social problems. Interfaith dialogue should not be the end but a tool to fight against those enemies of humanity, to keep hope alive, and to convert that hope into new realities.

**Planting the Seeds of Pluralism, Creating a Dialogue Network**

So, what can hope look like in Indonesia? In the eyes of Interfidei, a social dimension of hope is represented by the youth. When we look at the realities of religious violence, we see clearly that any type of peacemaking effort, including interfaith dialogue, must include the youth among the key players. Therefore, one of Interfidei's main projects is aimed at educating young people. Since 1998, when Soeharto was toppled from power, Interfidei has promoted a series of intensive short courses in religious studies. More recently these courses have been combined with workshops on pluralism, conflict, and peacemaking.[9] Initially, both programs were held mostly in Yogyakarta, where Interfidei is located. As an important historical city and the primary center of education in Indonesia, Yogyakarta is important for Interfidei. The brightest and most progressive students from all over Indonesia come to Yogyakarta and become some of our best partners.

Interfidei's research department designs curriculum for its classes and updates it as necessary. A class usually consists of ten to twenty-five participants and meets every week for four to five weeks at Interfidei's office. Most participants are college students whose studies span diverse disciplines, from theology to computer sciences. The instructors are either scholars or religious leaders invited from each of the faith traditions covered in the course. Initially, a short course focused on the history, theology, and ethics of each religious tradition. In later developments, the curriculum began to emphasize the relationships between religion and power, religion and human rights, religion and gender, issues concerning religious education, and explorations of the relationship of religion to many other contemporary issues.

With its success in Yogyakarta, invitations came from other cities and local communities. Interfidei grew and began to hold the same program in many other "strategic" cities all over Indonesia. When held outside Yogyakarta, the course meets intensively every day for four to five days. For any program held outside Yogyakarta, Interfidei always relies upon its local network. Topic, venue, participants, organizers, budget, speakers, and other concerns are always based on mutual agreement between Interfidei and its local partner. That way, Interfidei can offer a program relevant to the actual needs of a local community and can network with the existing local interfaith organization in a way that builds mutual trust. This kind of effective collaboration between Interfidei members and the local interfaith organization has apparently made joining the program much more attractive to local people.

There are critical considerations that we in Interfidei must undertake in deciding where to hold a course or other program. For example, we often look for locations that have strong conflict potential or that have just been struck by a conflict. In the areas that have a strong potential for conflict our course is designed for prevention, while in post-conflict areas our curriculum is designed to be part of conflict-resolution. Another critical consideration concerns the degree of education of our participants. In Yogyakarta most of the participants are college students; in most areas outside Java Island the level of education is lower, and few young people go to college. One dilemma we face is that our short course is frequently mischaracterized as an "academic" program, and thus young people with "better" education are more likely to attend, and those with less education are not. This can be both a plus and a minus of the program. It is a plus, because the program attracts more of the best educated young people, who will play important roles in any hoped-for social transformation. Also, most of the participants are individuals who already have some interest in religious pluralism. But it can be a minus, since the less-well-educated and also the older generation are not accommodated.

Two important points are always emphasized by Interfidei through its programs. First, we strongly encourage participants to create their own interfaith group or join an existing group after the program is over. We want the students to learn how to network and promote interfaith dialogue to the wider public. Moreover, if what we believe is true, we know that they can reach out and find friends who will respond to our message and join. Second, we want our interfaith-dialogue movement to be an integral part of the necessary social transformation and the democratization process in Indonesia. We have faith that, by fostering open and sincere conversation and opportunities for cooperative social interaction, we can promote collaboration among people of different religions and make a wonderful contribution toward the true civil society.

As a result of the Interfidei programs, in 1999 two interfaith organizations were founded by our alumni in Manado (North Sulawesi) and Makassar (South Sulawesi). In 2000, our alumni in Banjarmasin (South Borneo) established a similar organization, followed by other groups of alumni in Palangkaraya (Central Borneo) and in Kupang (Eastern Indonesia) in the following year. The same is the case with our alumni in Sumatera, Java, and some other parts of the country. In the past few years, each of these interfaith organizations has grown and multiplied. A further exciting development is that each group has begun to focus on a particular interest, such as conflict-resolution, gender issues in religion, ethnic conflict prevention, peacebuilding, promoting tolerance, etc. Interfidei is happy to be part of this promising process. Building networks like these is crucial, not only because doing so multiplies our power efficiently, but also because it is impossible to engage in this huge task alone. Gradually, we can see that our hope for success is becoming more real.

Of course this success is not the whole story. Indonesia is still a patrimonial society where most religious community members view their religious leaders as patrons. The words and actions of religious leaders as patrons are very influential in relation to both peace and violence. Educating young people is very important, but it is not sufficient. Since religious leaders are key players, it is very important to create opportunities for them to sit down and talk to each other in order to clarify dangerous misconceptions, misunderstandings, and biases and to promote any possible collaboration among them and their people.

Interfidei's other primary program, the workshop on pluralism, conflict, and peace, can be particularly effective in this arena. The short course described above is more academic and suitable for young people who may be interested in religious pluralism and interfaith dialogue, while the workshop is more practical and fits the needs of both younger and older people, including religious leaders. Participants join the workshop because they are stakeholders in a society whose citizens need to find solutions for their common problems. Thus, participants in the workshop come from a very wide spectrum of backgrounds, ranging from members of the most exclusivist to the most pluralist groups, from very senior people to young people, from important civic figures to common householders. This diversity makes the workshop very dynamic and challenging at the same time.

Just like the short course, the workshop on pluralism is held by Interfidei in Yogyakarta and in many other cities all over Indonesia. When held outside Yogya, Interfidei again relies upon close collaboration with local interfaith communities. Thus, Interfidei will first come and consult with the local interfaith communities and key figures, including women and youth, to decide on a topic that is relevant to the existing issues. Sometimes, especially when tension is already in the air, personal meetings and visits are made to key figures first in order to promote wider participation. As instructors and facilitators, we have brought in academics, activists, and authoritative religious scholars whose work is relevant to the chosen workshop topic. We literally move into the community for several days. We stay in one place, eat the same food, share in the prayers, and witness how others practice each belief. Through this process we create friendships that are the basis of an interfaith community that shares not only stories and concerns but, most importantly, trust and mutual collaboration to overcome various common problems.

The workshop is a very exciting experience, held over four to five days. During the first day we ask participants to introduce themselves and share concerns, problems, and experiences related to the topic of the workshop. Then we break out into small groups to discuss some controversial issues. The following days unfold in a series of sessions that include question-and-answer time with our expert speakers. In the evenings we organize small-group discussions on topics related to the previous sessions; these are supervised by trained facilitators. The last day we offer an optional excursion to various historical sacred places, religious centers of education, museums, or local mosques, churches, temples, vihara, and the like. The concluding session is one of evaluation and reflection, including an exchange of messages and hopes among the participants and staff. Some of the papers presented at the workshops eventually are published in books.

Obviously, when we work in areas of the country that are rife with conflict, this kind of interfaith encounter begins full of tension and suspicion.[10] In a critically tense time, even a small thing from the "other" side can be seen as suspicious, if not dangerous. Here, Interfidei as an interfaith-dialogue organization with members from different religious backgrounds sometimes faces a dilemma. From the perspective of both conflicting groups, Interfidei can be seen as friend of the enemy—and a friend of the enemy is the enemy. Muslims sometimes see Interfidei as a Christian organization with a mission to evangelize. It happens that many key figures of our organization are Christians. So Interfidei can be seen as a Christian agency whose purpose is to poison Muslim minds, especially the youth, with western ideas and ideology for the sake of a Christian agenda. Even the use of a candle as Interfidei's logo is suspect for some Muslims. For them, a candle is identical to Christianity. Christians can view Interfidei as an Islamic organization whose ultimate mission is to make Indonesia an Islamic state. They make their assumption based on seeing the strong presence of Muslim members and female staff (including my wife) who wear the Islamic scarf. Christian members of Interfidei are seen as either not true Christians or as puppet figures used by Muslims to domesticate the rest of the Christian population. Only through a dedicated and often uneasy process of respectful speech and deep listening does each group gradually learn more and more about and from the "other."

The following stories from workshops held in Makassar, South Sulawesi, in 2001 and in Palangkaraya, East Borneo, in 2002 are interesting and perhaps instructive. On the first day when participants introduced themselves to each other and shared some experiences and concerns, two participants decided to leave the forum. Why? The incident was triggered by a debate between some members of the Muslim and Christian groups on the difficulties faced by Christians who want to build a new church in almost any part of the country.[11] Two members of a right-wing Islamic group totally rejected any argument from Christian members. "This is Christianization!" they shouted in an explosive tone. One of them slammed the table and walked out, followed by his friend. Everyone else was shocked by that very emotionally tense moment.

Some of our Muslim members went after them to talk in private and were able to convince those two participants to listen. Eventually, by evening, they came back to the room. They then stayed until the last day of the workshop! We are not strangers to tension, and we have had to learn how to work through many obstacles. We discuss. We share our fears and hopes. We learn together and create friendships. It was all of this good work, but especially the friendships that grew among the participants in the remaining sessions, that enabled the man who slammed the table to change his attitude gradually. In the concluding session, he spoke of his regret and apologized for what he did on the first day. In addition, he has now become a committed interfaith activist and part of Interfidei's network in Makassar.

On the last day of a workshop in Palangkaraya, certain participants were enraged when, as written in our schedule, we informed the group to get ready for a visit to a Catholic church. All of a sudden one of them strongly protested the trip and walked out, slamming the door behind him; friends quickly followed him. They returned when reminded that the visit was optional and even decided to go along with the group, "but we don't want to enter the church," they said. So, they walked around outside while the group was in the church listening to the tour guide. Before the group left, some of the Muslim members who had been inside the church started to tease those who had refused to go in. Eventually, perhaps out of curiosity or shame, some of them snuck into the church and took pictures. On the trip back they poked fun at each other. Slowly but surely, their suspicion and unfriendly attitude toward non-Muslim acquaintancess disappeared. In many cases, it is from these informal situations that true friendships grow naturally and wipe out mutual suspicion.

The issue of erecting a church (or any minority's house of worship) in a Muslim neighborhood needs a little more elaboration here. Many Muslims assume that the way a church or other faith's house of worship gets organized is the same as a mosque's. Since every Muslim can go and pray in any mosque, so should a Christian. Just like Muslims, Christians should naturally go to the churches closest to their homes and should not be allowed to build a church in a neighborhood where only one or two Christian families live. Thus, if Christians keep building churches in neighborhoods where only one Christian family lives, this is surely a thinly disguised and well-planned strategy of Christianization! Muslims can only understand what creating new churches might mean when they understand the "logic" of Christian denominations.

Sometimes we encounter religious leaders who, out of ignorance or malice, interpret the doctrine or the scripture of the other's religion based on their own bias. Or, they compare what is historical and actual in other religions to what is theological and thus ideal in their religion. [12] When this happens, we bring in a "pluralist" scholar to give an alternative interpretation and teach the doctrine or scripture in another way. Clearly, not everyone can agree, but, again, through hard work, eventually many can transform themselves, especially after an experience of true friendship. In fact, an encounter of friendship can become an opportunity to see both the "self" and "the other" very differently. We found, for example, that some Muslim members are gradually able to enjoy the sound of a church bell as a call for remembering God, not as the disturbing noise from the infidel's house of worship, as it was perceived before. Likewise, Christians can also enjoy the melody of *adzan*, the Islamic call for prayer, which is simultaneously aired by hundreds of loudspeakers from the mosques at every corner of the block at the time of prayer, five times a day, including the one heard very early in the morning.

Clarification of Muslims' misperceptions of the Trinity and of Christians' misunderstandings of *jihad* are among other "popular" examples that we found helpful in overcoming mutual suspicion and animosity. From the workshop many Christians learned that mainstream Indonesian Muslims do not want to make the country an Islamic state through the scary word, "*jihad*." At the same time, Muslims learned that Christians are not literally worshiping three gods whose main agenda is to Christianize the whole world. People from each group also learned that there is surprising diversity in other traditions and that each has similar internal problems.

The encouraging result of participating in these workshops is that many agree to see their commonalities, and even their problems and concerns, as opportunities for collaboration rather than as points of conflict. Muslim groups now realize that the difficulties faced by Christians, Hindus, and other religious groups in establishing houses of worship in the majority Muslim neighborhood are also experienced by Muslims who live in non-Muslim neighborhoods. As a result, more and more people from each group now realize the urgency of abolishing the government regulation on the matter. In fact, they now see how discriminatory rules like this one frequently result in horizontal conflict among religious groups and also can be easily manipulated to benefit particular political interests.

In February, 2003, Interfidei held a seminar and workshop on "Religion and Violence." Attended by interfaith activists from all over the country, this meeting carefully studied real problems related to conflict potential, public policy, and effective networking strategies. They formed agreements to collaborate on projects to eliminate religious discrimination and on programs to empower the local interfaith-dialogue organizations.[13]

One further interfaith group that Interfidei initially facilitated is a community of teachers of religion. Thanks to the sponsorship of Oslo Coalition Norway in 2004–06, Interfidei conducted a research project on the teaching of religion in public schools, from elementary to high-school levels. The researchers discovered the existing curriculum to be deficient on many levels and that students are not being prepared how to respond appropriately to the plurality of religions in Indonesia. Interfidei followed up by offering training programs for teachers on religious pluralism. Participants in the training now regularly meet with each other to share concerns, information, and experiences. A newsletter called "Dharma-Bhakti" (dedication) was published in order to share what they learned with a wider audience. Some of the most committed teachers of religion organized themselves as a group called "Liberal Teachers."

It is through efforts like these that Interfidei plants the seeds of the values of religious pluralism. We hope and believe that there will come a time when these seeds sprout and offer humanity much beauty and wisdom.

## Conclusion

Short courses in religious studies and serial workshops on pluralism, conflict, and peace are Interfidei's two most successful interfaith-dialogue programs at the grass roots in Indonesia. As illustrated above, contributing to the success of Interfidei's programs are the diverse models through which Interfidei presents its message, networks, and encourages participation. Interfidei's strength is its ability to reframe points of conflict into problems that are newly understood as held in common. Interfidei places importance on practicing interfaith dialogue in the service of a global social transformation. In the interpersonal realm, of course, the basis for all the work is fostering genuine friendship.

Interfaith dialogue may begin with a public forum, a course, or a teaching, but for us the real dialogue should eventually become a warm encounter among people. Our real work is to promote enlightened and respectful interfaith conversation among friends and family members. This work is much more than just a conversation of ideas, doctrine, or theology. The best interfaith-dialogue organization—and this is true also of a society, a nation, and even our whole globe—should be like a shared home where each family member can have privacy in his or her room but also have public space in which one may speak freely and fully about any common problem—and thus cooperate in making the space a safe and comfortable home for everyone.

## Notes

1. I am grateful to Wiwin St. Aminah Rohmawati, my wife and the former Executive Secretary of Interfidei, as well as to Elga Sarapung, the Executive Director of Interfidei, for reading the first draft of this essay and providing me with valuable input and information.

2. On July 26–29, 2005, MUI (Majelis Ulama Indonesia) held its seventh national meeting and issued eleven fatwas (religious edicts). One of its controversial decrees says that religious pluralism, liberalism, and secularism are prohibited (*haram*) in Islam. See MUI's decree number 7/MUNAS VII/MUI/II/2005.

3. For more on Institut DIAN/Interfidei, please visit: http://www.interfidei.or.id/ or read the special edition of *Newsletter Interfidei* "On Interfidei," April, 1998. On Th. Sumartana, read *Newsletter Interfidei,* no. 15/VII, January–March, 2003, a special edition to commemorate his death that year. We at Interfidei prefer the term "interfaith" to emphasize the essential aspect of religion as well as common concern of individual believers; "interreligious" focuses more on religion as institution. See Fatimah Husein, *Muslim-Christian Relations in the New Order Indonesia, the Exclusivist and Inclusivist Muslims' Perspectives* (Bandung: Mizan, 2005), p. 272.

4. Triggered by a regional monetary crisis that began in July, 1997, in Thailand, Indonesia was severely hit by economic crisis in 1997–98. The economy collapsed, and Soeharto, who had held power for more than three decades, was forced to step down. This critical era is known as the "Reformasi" period, a highly uncertain situation signified by dysfunction and disorientation of many aspects of social life. Additional natural disasters have also contributed to Indonesia's struggle: the tsunami in Sumatra that took over 200,000 lives in 2004, the earthquake in Yogyakarta that killed more than 6,000 people in 2006, and

floods and landslides in other parts of the country.

5. According to the 2000 census data from BPS-Statistics Indonesia, Christians constitute roughly 9% of the population, Hindus about 2%, and Buddhists 1%. The other 2% consists of practitioners of indigenous beliefs, Confucianism, Baha'ism, Sikhism, and other religions, including a tiny Jewish community in Surabaya, East Java, with the only synagogue in the country. Ethnic-religious stereotyping also creates confusion: Malay, Bugises or Madurese are mistaken for Muslims, and Batak, Dayak, or Ambon are mistaken for Christians. As a result, a personal quarrel between a Bugise and an Ambonese can be immediately transformed into Muslim-Christian conflict, involving more people wrongly.

6. Th. Sumartana, "Some Issues and Challenges for Plural Society, A Reflection on the Experiences of Interfidei," a paper presented to an international conference on "Living in Pluralistic Society" held by the British Council in Jakarta, February 22–23, 2002.

7. Leonard Swidler, *After the Absolute: The Dialogical Future of Religious Reflection* (Minneapolis, MN: Fortress Press, 1990), p. 43.

8. To read about other ethnic and interfaith violence in Indonesia, see, e.g., Mochtar Mas'oed, *Kekerasan Kolektif, Kondisi dan Pemicu* (Yogyakarta: P3PK-UGM, 2001).

9. In Indonesia, students from elementary school to university are required to take courses in religion, focusing on their own tradition. Therefore, most students are ignorant about religions other than their own; consequently, misunderstanding, misconception, and mutual suspicion feed the existing religious conflict and violence. Studying a different religious tradition is a rare opportunity. In 2003, a regulation of the Indonesian Education System required every educational institution to provide religious instruction according to the religion of the student. Many Christian schools protested what they say as a "hidden agenda." After pressure from some Muslim groups, the regulation was implemented. Complicated and unresolved problems have followed.

10. Poso, Central Sulawesi, experienced at least three rounds of Muslim-Christian conflict in 1998, 2000, and 2006. Pontianak and Sambas, West Borneo, experienced horrible ethnic conflict between the Dayaks and the Madurese in 1996. Ambon and Maluku were torn by bloody Muslim-Christian conflicts in 1999–2002.

11. According to decree, a house of worship can only by renovated or built when sixty people who live in the neighborhood agree (Letter of Mutual Agreement between the Ministsry of Religious Affairs and the Ministry of Domestic Affairs, Numbers 1/8/9, 1969 on the Implementation of Governmental Apparatus in Enforcing the Safety and Security of Religious Groups and their Practices). At least twenty-two houses of worship belonging to various minority groups were closed down during 2007. See *Report on Freedom of Religion and Belief in Indonesia* (Jakarta: SETARA Institute, 2007), p. 11.

12. Goddard calls this a "double standard," i.e., comparing what is good in us to what is bad in others. Clearly, the result is misunderstanding and misjudgment. See Hugh Goddard, *Christians and Muslims: From Double Standard to Mutual Understanding* (London: Routledge, 1995).

13. Gedong Ashram Gandi in Candi Dasa, Bali, is an interfaith community founded in 1976 by Gedong Bagus Oka, a prominent Indonesian female Hindu thinker and humanitarian activist. She was a founding member, Vice President, and Honorary President of the World Conference on Religion and Peace. For further information about programs mentioned here, see the *Report on Candi Dasa Meeting* (Yogyakarta: Institut DIAN/ Interfidei, 2003).

*Epilogue*

# FRIENDSHIP COUNTS MOST
Marcia Prager and Rebecca Kratz Mays

**Marcia's Story**

The room is filled with light and silence. A complete quiet, yet the stillness is not one of absence, but of deep presence. Eyes are closed, hands gently held in a chain that encircles and unites all in the room. This occasion may seem like the opening meditation of a Jewish Renewal *davvenen'*, but it isn't. It is a Quaker gathering, and I am for some a now familiar guest. For others, this is their first gathering (known in Quaker circles as a "Meeting") led not by a Friend but by a rabbi.

We have been in silence for some time now. I begin a soft, wordless melody, a *niggun*, while gently squeezing the hands I hold. The squeeze pulses in a chain around the room, each person calling the next back from their private meditation. The *niggun* continues. It moves through the room, building in intentionality and in intensity.

For Meeting, this is not the norm. Prepared for the challenge of introducing customs so different from Quaker practice, I had spoken briefly, ahead of time, about my joy in being able to share wisdom from the Jewish spiritual path with a community that has come to feel like a second home to me. I'd told them that I'd go with them into silence (wow, is sustained silence hard for Jews!), and that we'd come out of the silence, not to talking, but into melody. A *niggun*, a wordless melody in my people's tradition, serves a comparable role to that of silence for Quakers: a wordless vehicle crafted to carry us to deep centers of awareness and new possibilities for self-reflection and spiritual deepening. Within a *niggun*, we can open our hearts to feel life most deeply. We travel again to the places in our souls that hurt and the places that sing with joy. Sometimes, if we are willing, those can merge, and a great unifying light envelopes us. We feel an exaltation and a nurturing love. We are lifted up, and along with us the melody floats higher and higher.

For a community that has foresworn ritual, liturgy, and (to large

121

measure) even song, this experience is new. Being no strangers to the journey within, however, in only a few moments every voice has joined. The *niggun* flows like a river. I model "hand-dancing," beating the rhythm on knees, clapping, raising arms like branches toward heaven, bringing hands inward toward the heart. With eyes closed, a *niggun* can be traveled far and deep. I invite all who wish to do so to close their eyes, seated or standing, and intensify the *niggun*. With eyes closed we are alone while not alone, in private space yet aware of and supported by the presence of those around us. Later, after sharing more Jewish story and teaching, I will ask if anyone wishes to share their experience. I know the responses will be wonderful. This is a community of seekers who welcome challenge and appreciate genuine spiritual work. While the Jewish idiom may be new, the style uncustomary, they are not new either to the quest for God within and beyond or to the voice that calls us to be agents of God in the world.

How did this interfaith journey, which has brought me into the heart of Quaker faith and practice, begin? These days "Interreligious Dialogue" is an entire discipline; yet, sometimes, as in my case, the door to a life of dialogue opens un-sought-for. It comes as a gift that can only be acknowledged in retrospect as yet one more evidence of Divine Grace.

It was shortly after I had completed my studies at the Reconstructionist Rabbinical College. Newly ordained, I nevertheless continued my studies with my most beloved teacher and mentor, Rabbi Zalman Schachter-Shalomi. One of Reb Zalman's greatest gifts to his students is his willingness to assign and empower us to go out to teach, lead, and create those opportunities that would support our own emergence into leadership. He never hoarded his own well-earned leadership role but shared it with the loving wisdom of a great mentor. Therefore, the day he called me to announce that he was sending me instead of himself to Germantown Friends Meeting to do a Sunday morning teaching on Jewish mysticism and spiritual practice, "Yes" was the best and only answer. Little did I know how that one "yes" would change my life.

So there I was, at Germantown Friends Meeting, having read as much about Quaker faith and practice as the few days' notice would permit, floating a *niggun* into the silence, and teaching Jewish wisdom about Light, Love, and Oneness. That morning I fell in love with the Quaker path and met those key individuals whose roles in my life would change my life forever. I stepped, with the kind of blissful unawareness of a neophyte, into a life of radical interfaith dialogue that would unfold stunning insights, push me way past whatever I thought was my comfort zone, and stretch my heart to hold more compassion than I could ever have imagined. That morning I met Howard Lesnick, who would later help me give birth to the book I only imagined that I might write, and Carolyn Coates, who proved to be an even more gifted *shadchan* (matchmaker) than she could ever have envisioned. It was she who so gently but insistently suggested that I teach at the Friends General Conference and that I meet Rebecca Mays.

## Rebecca's Story

"Interfaith" encounters began quite young for me in my large Southern Baptist congregation in Dallas, Texas. About age nine, I participated in a religious education class where each week we met and learned from adherents to other faith practices: Mormons, Catholics, Seventh-day Adventists, and Jews. I sat riveted, captivated by the differences and wondering where my fresh experience of immersion baptism fit. I still glowed with the sense of blessing and belonging I had felt as I was baptized and accepted into the church community of devout believers.

The class was intended to lend support to new converts like me, strengthening our ability to understand the step into a faith commitment we had taken by understanding the differences. At the time I felt cared for and that my step in faith meant something important beyond my own experience. Both such gifts are extremely important to young people, and I owe a debt of gratitude to my parents and that church for giving me such gifts at such a tender time.

In my thirties, I found two specific memories from that class returning during times of prayer. The first was a sense of awe I had experienced in pondering a God who could create all these different variations on encountering that loving presence that led me to be baptized. Second, I could recall in intricate detail the two rabbis who had come to teach us of Judaism—their warmth and love for God had felt so similar to what I had glimpsed in my own nascent turning to God.

But now, twenty-five years later, why was this memory returning so strongly? My college experience at Earlham College had led me to join the Religious Society of Friends. I had studied my Anabaptist roots in graduate school, seeking to understand better my Christian heritage. At the urging of this vibrant childhood memory, I realized the time had come to meet Jesus as Jewish. I had taken a long time even to register the historical truth that he had lived as a Jew. I was scared to enter what felt unfamiliar; even more, I even worried that I might be "doing wrong" to cross a boundary that defined my identity as a Christian. But I had a burning question that I felt God had placed in my heart; what could I learn about this dear Jesus of mine from seeing what it meant to be Jewish? I felt that, if I could understand his Jewish practices, then I might actually know him better as my personal Savior. I wanted to learn how and when these two traditions had parted company and why. So I tucked the fear of becoming disoriented in my faith into prayer. When I had left the Baptists to join the Quakers, I had done the same, trusting that if this God I worshiped was as omniscient as I chose to believe, then my trust would enlarge, and I would know more of the union with God I sought. So, whether just plain curiosity or that desire for union or both, something pulled me, and I followed to the door of Marcia's home.

## Marcia's Story

The day I met Rebecca started out like an ordinary day. All my days were filled with students who came for lessons, couples and individuals who came for counseling, and this or that person who showed up seeking some bit of Jewish wisdom on one subject or another. Only later did I learn how long Rebecca stood on the porch, gathering her courage to knock on the door. I suspect that she also knew that stepping through that doorway would change her life forever.

Rebecca stayed that day for hours. We shared the stories of our lives, looking to find that *telos* toward which Carolyn Coates's intuition was supposed to lead us. Rebecca was a convinced Quaker, brought up not in the (for me reasonably comfortable) liberal Quaker world, which was now her spiritual home, but in the South—a Southern Baptist, with all the Billy Graham trimmings. She was, O My God, a Christian! I mean a real Christian whose personal savior was Jesus. And I was a Jewish rabbi, whose Eastern European immigrant grandparents never left the *shtetl* of Brooklyn and who had implanted their memories of pogroms and Christian violence in their children's and grandchildren's memory banks as vividly as in their own.

Keep breathing. Had I not, with all the fascination that the forbidden "other" holds for any of us, been secretly reading the Gospels for years? Had I not read every biography of Jesus, both historical and fictional (and everything in between), that I could lay my hands on? Had I not, in my own way, long ago come to terms with a Jesus I could relate to: a first-century Jewish itinerant rebbe, teacher, rabble-rouser, healer, counselor, and guide for the poor, the alienated, and the oppressed? His essential message was familiar to me from that of other great rabbis of the time. Hadn't Hillel already taught the same *Torah*: Listen Israel, the Infinite One Whose Name is the Breath of Life is our God and Guide, The Infinite One is a true Unity, and you must love that One who is your God, with all your passion, with every breath, with every fiber of your being; and you must love your fellow person as yourself.

And further: I had already discovered that by reading the Gospels in the Peshita—the Hebrew and Aramaic translations preserved by the Aramaic-speaking Christians of Syria—I could find in these "Christian" scriptures a deeply familiar style of Jewish midrashic literature. I could, for instance, read what Christians called the Lord's Prayer and see artfully sequenced segments drawn from the most familiar of Jewish prayers. In the "Beatitudes" I could find a great improvisational Jewish liturgist riffing on Ashrei, a liturgical form that expands on the "Fortunate are those who—" verses in Psalms. Thus, in the Peshita, I encountered a Jesus I could meet as a friend.

So here was Rebecca, a born-again Christian baptized by Wally Amos Criswell, a most conservative Southern Baptist minister; she was now a Quaker and still in love with Jesus. *Gevalt!*

**Rebecca's Story**

We discovered together, Marcia and I, a healing path for some of the pain that the history of violence between Christians and Jews had left us. We looked hard at the ways in which that history had hardened over millennia into offensive and defensive teachings of successionism, triumphalism, and all kinds of projections that our traditions have used to segregate and protect ourselves from the feared "other." Together we revisited the workshops we had each facilitated at a 1992 Quaker gathering where we had simply crossed paths in the dining room. There, at the Friends General Conference, Marcia had led a week-long workshop titled "*Ahavah Rabbah*: With a Great Love You Have Loved Us." I had facilitated one on how a person of faith could hold a particular faith and still be open to "the other"—a significant contribution I believe Quaker theology offers to all interfaith-dialogue efforts.

In her work, Marcia blended storytelling, movement, meditation, and song to enter the Jewish experience of *Ahavah* (Divine Love), *Chased* (Divine Grace), and *Rachamin* (Divine Compassion). In mine, I used open-ended, Socratic-like queries developed by my teacher and mentor, Mary Morrison, to liberate the synoptic Gospels. Marcia and I spent hours in her study teaching the content of these workshops to one another. It was a spirit-filled time, a journey of discovery. Together we found and deepened our mutual commitment to the One God moving within us and beyond us to redeem our world with an outpouring of Divine Love that calls us to make peace and justice real.

I had been teaching a course on the Gospels at Pendle Hill, a Quaker center for study and contemplation near Philadelphia. I invited Marcia to come to that class and teach the Lord's Prayer as a Jewish prayer.

## Marcia's Story

In the safe environment of Rebecca's course, I began to teach the Gospels in public for the first time. I shared Jewish readings of Jesus' teachings, placing them in a Jewish spiritual and liturgical context. Together in the class we worked on the Lord's Prayer, using the Hebrew and Aramaic as doorways beyond the English and Greek translations into the depths of Jewish wisdom. How wonderful to offer the Lord's Prayer, so unknown to Jews and so poorly translated for Christians, as a gem-like *t'fillah b'kitzur*, a profound and poetic condensation of major themes of traditional Jewish prayer. And also, in her course I encountered an opening to Quakerism and to Christianity that filled my soul with light.

The work deepened. We began to design entire courses, workshops, and retreats we could teach together. One summer at Pendle Hill, Rebecca and I led a four-day workshop: "Mystery and Commandment: Opening to Awe and Emerging to Action." We designed a Quaker Christian-Jewish Renewal exploration of our unique and shared experiences of "being called," drawing from both Jewish and Quaker traditions about experiencing awe and affirming right action. We began to travel to teach together, accepting invitations from churches and retreat centers to take our Quaker/Christian/Jewish dialogue beyond Pendle Hill and Philadelphia.

At the same time, naturally, our personal dialogue deepened. Like loving companions who gradually reveal more of their hopes and fears to each other, we began to explore not only how the spiritual wisdom of our respective paths complemented each other but also where they did not. We had to learn new vocabularies for the discourse, as we had such different ways of languaging our experiences. We sometimes had to unpack critically divergent nuances of meaning with hours of explanation. There were so few words that we used with the same intention. What is redemption? What is sin? What is messiah? What is the Bible? Is that the same as Torah? What is the cross? What are prayer, repentance, resurrection, life-after-death? What is fact? What is truth? When are they the same, and when not? Why do Jews and Christians read the same texts so differently? What are the pitfalls of translation? Who was

Jesus? Was he a mortal "son of man" or a divine one? Did he die before he could even possibly become a messiah or die in order to be one?

## Rebecca's Story

At times along the way, I had to "slow down." I felt I couldn't stretch any more at the risk of losing touch with my own spiritual path and formation. I remembered the wisdom of the Greek philosopher, Plotinus. He used the image of a wheel to describe how to encounter radical differences among religions. Each tradition, he said, is like a spoke on the wheel, with God's love and truth at the hub. As we move through our daily lives, turning round the circumference, the spokes need to hold firm. Through study, prayer, and reflection, we plumb our own particular traditions, circumstances, and spiritual experiences. In doing so, we can travel inward along a spoke toward the center of the wheel. From there we then can see "that of God" in the person who has traveled toward the center along a different spoke. We cannot render the differences facile; their subtleties will reveal more of God to us if we are open to them. Each time I couldn't stretch any larger, I knew the time had come to study within my own Christian/Quaker context again. In those more internal times, I also came to recognize one of the many layers of "stretching" that had been happening in our work together.

Beginning with the Jewish *niggun* and the Quaker silence, a rich and expansive story of encounter has grown for Marcia and me. It now includes many other people who are moved to bring alive those qualities of authentic worship that can empower peace and justice in our time. Patience and passion are both needed for the long journey. Both words come from the same Latin root meaning "to suffer with." The use of the word "suffer" here means simply "bear with" or "accompany" with both the sense of intensity in passion and the sense of quiet, expectant waiting in patience. We do this interreligious dialogue work accompanying God, in the trust and patience that God's reconciling nature is at work even when we do not see it; we do it with the passion that bears with the intensity of the need to help make a difference now.

With patience and passion, new understanding comes as well as the compassion born of becoming friends.

At Pendle Hill, among the many retreats that Marcia and I led together was the one we called "Mystery and Commandment." Along with about twenty other seekers we studied the Torah story of Jacob's wrestling with the angel. Alongside that story, we entered the Gospel of Luke's account of

Mary's resistance to the news from the angel Gabriel that she would bear a child, a son of God, who would be called Jesus or, more accurately, Yeshua.

In our parallel study of these texts, we explored the inner landscape of encounter between humanity and divinity. I could feel my own awe in the power of powerlessness—as each one yielded to a new understanding of herself or himself with God. I rediscovered the joy of yielding my own ego-sense of my "rights," my purely personal choices, on behalf of something vastly larger: a faith tradition, a people, a sense of call. I understood better the counsel of that Anabaptist Hutterite friend who said: "As an individual we are entitled to all our human rights; as a communal people, we are not, however, entitled to exercise all of them any time we choose." Jacob and Mary had each taken a step. Their engagement with God did not diminish their individuality but made their capacity to live into the Presence so much larger. I had discovered more of the depth of my own Christian identity by encountering more of the depth of my Hebrew spiritual ancestors.

Another time, Marcia and I were guests at a pastors' conference sponsored by the Billy Graham Association. Yes. Rabbi Marcia and I went together to a week-long training program for evangelical, born-again Christian ministers. Marcia chuckles sometimes when she points to her suitable-for-framing certificate of graduation from the training, as surely she is the only rabbi ever to have received one. I was happy to be there, enjoying a return to that community of faith that had so nourished me and still felt so familiar. I knew Marcia was my willing companion but obviously cautious and prepared to be confronted with an unwelcome theology and style of worship.

We came to this community of pastors to learn about their faith, their lives, and their concerns and to share ours when invited. I felt I might be able to speak of my own journey away from evangelical fundamentalism from an insider's perspective, using our common language to share my enlarged understanding of Christianity. I also wanted them to meet a rabbi whose respect for Christianity was strong and who might also be able to offer a point of view that could help break through stereotypes and open up more expansive ways of understanding Jews and Judaism. We had discussed all these hopes with the planners; we were invited to come with scholarship help and were received with great hospitality.

At the heart of their concerns was one that brought Marcia and me to another teachable moment in the adventure of doing interreligious dialogue. In every message, from the big-screen, larger-than-life videocasts to the pounding gospel rock, and infusing each pastor's own religious life, was the message that charged the conference with its passion: the ultimate, atoning, saving power of Jesus' death on the cross. This message had charged my own life with passion for years, and now I was reweaving its meaning for myself, allowing gentleness and kindness to be the measure of my passion for an authentic encounter with God that reaches into the heart and changes us. The language to describe this encounter can sometimes create misunderstandings, but as Marcia and I allowed ourselves to sink beneath the language into the sensation of being touched and called by that Power, we found that we could share rich times of prayer with those we met.

We were brought to a moment of quiet with one another at breakfast one morning. We conversed gently about the atonement, knowing it was an uncomfortable place for each of us for different reasons. I had often heard Marcia's teaching from Torah about Abraham and the angel who had intervened to relieve Abraham from having to slay his son. We spoke about Jesus on the cross as being like Isaac on the altar of stones, willing to give his life if that was what God wanted. She stretched again to understand what was so fundamentally true to me: the power in my own life of the saving power of Jesus' choice to surrender his life. I was brought again to the quiet where no easy intellectual reconciliation came.

Grounded in my deeply schooled Quaker respect for active silence before the mystery of God's wholeness, I could only slip into prayer and let the mystery of the difference be, trusting I need not fear it or change it. At that moment, Marcia spoke with warmth and compassion, "I'm just sad the angel didn't intervene." For a moment, I felt the threat of difference, the threat of my story's having no meaning if we couldn't agree on the atoning power of Jesus' life. Even agreeing to disagree and respect one another felt flat. Then the sense of peace returned, and I could just trust the differences and the compassion we each had for the other and what God had in mind. My path with Jesus had been strengthened and deepened for learning more of Torah. My faith was not threatened; I was only invited into greater trust. I became more and more clear of an active and awesome Presence that finds each of us where we are and loves us with an unending love. I also became aware of how important the trust of a deep friendship can be as the foundation for the long-term work of doing interreligious dialogue. I grew in my respect for what Marcia's experience among Christians and Quakers was like.

## Marcia's Story

I have been told that the Society of Friends estimates that twenty percent of Quakers are Jews. When I teach in Quaker meetings and other gatherings, I rarely need to ask who the Jews are. I usually see that you are crying as I speak. Afterwards you wait until the other well-wishers have spoken to me and are gone, and you come up to me on the path or in the hall to tell me about how much you appreciate my being there and how much the Jewish you still hurts. I often hear you say that you have never, until now, heard a Jewish teacher speak of love or the heart, of the feminine as part of God, of *mitzvot* having spiritual substance, of Judaism as a deep spiritual path. You tell stories of bad teaching and insensitive counseling that break my heart. I hear you tell me that the Quaker community has been a place of solace and refuge, of peace and growth, and that even after so many years my offering reminds you how deep is the pain that remains. You ask me: Do I have a congregation? Are there other rabbis who teach as I do? Can you remain a Quaker and still find a way to be a Jew? Is there a way to be a Jew for someone like you?

Then I speak of the Jewish Renewal movement and the new forms of Jewish spirituality that are emerging and re-emerging, of the new role of women in spiritual leadership, of new songs and prayers, and of the renewed deepening of our connection to Torah, Kabbalah, and our people's ancient wisdom. I speak of a new community of inclusivity, of the great homecoming that is happening that does not ask us to discard, but rather to integrate, all that we have learned on the other spiritual paths we've traveled when we were not spiritually nourished at home. Finally, I speak of the healing of the Jewish soul work that our generation is called upon to do. We are a people that has internalized waves of trauma throughout our history. To be spiritually open means opening wounds to risk healing. To be healers we must nurture compassion. This is our great task. I invite you to think of yourself as already having begun to walk that path.

I am deeply moved by the openness to Jewish teaching that every Quaker gathering I've visited has shown me. As a community, the Quakers have allowed me to speak from an explicitly Jewish vantage point about the most profound challenges of the spiritual quest. As Georgia Peters of Pendle Hill wrote in an open letter after my session there called "Images and Names for God," "I am in a time of exploration concerning the issue of Christology. What Rabbi Prager did was to take me underneath all those questions to the basic faith experience. I was not bound up in an either/or frame of mind about Judaism and Christianity but saw their commonalities and new modes for the growth of my own faith."

I want to close my part of this essay with a blessing. The first part of the blessing is for all those Jews who have found a sustaining and nourishing spirituality in the Quaker house: *May this be for good and for blessing. May your* neshamas/*souls bring blessing to all those who have offered you* welcome. *May the respite and time for healing you have found come back to us. May you come home with wisdom, love, compassion, and renewed hope.*

For Quakers of all origins: *May your faith deepen and be a source of strength and joy. Yours is a path that welcomes all seekers with serenity and grace. Be blessed.*

For Jews: *Now is a time for us to heal so we can go forward with the enlightened of all peoples toward the One Light. May we deepen our Torah. May we open our hearts, welcoming home all who have sought elsewhere for so long. May we have the courage to craft for them and for us a fitting vessel, deeply rooted in the historic wisdom of our people and reaching also to the future.*

### From Marcia and Rebecca, a Blessing for All of Us:

*May we all have the loving strength to share the deep spiritual wisdom and inspired guidance of our paths with one another, neither defensively nor triumphally, but from a centered place of wholeness and peace. Amen.*